The Gardener's Spirit

30 Days of Heart & Humor *for the* Gardener

Theresa A. Markham

Copyright © 2025 by Theresa A. Markham

All rights reserved.

No part of this publication may be reproduced, distributed, or transmitted in any form or by any means, including photocopying, recording, or other electronic or mechanical methods, without the prior written permission of the publisher, except as permitted by U.S. copyright law. For permission requests, contact Theresa A. Markham at Theresa@TheresaMarkham.com.

ISBN: 979-8-9897120-0-7

Published by
Road Trip Books
4 Sundance Ter
Hamburg, NJ 07419
Road-Trip-Books.com

Dedicated to the love of my life, Chuck,
for his endless love and support,
and for Flying Me to the Moon.

And for John,
who generously allowed me to garden in his field,
without whom this book would never
have been possible.

TABLE OF CONTENTS

INTRODUCTION* 1
Aristotle 5
DAY 1: Optimism 7
DAY 2: Notes 13
DAY 3: Adaptation 19
DAY 4: Coffee 25
DAY 5: Restored 31
DAY 6: Big Rocks 35
DAY 7: Small Rocks 41
DAY 8: Gloves 47
DAY 9: T-shirts 53
DAY 10: Rain 57
Aristotle 63
DAY 11: Earthworms 65
DAY 12: Grasshoppers 71
DAY 13: Mystery 77
DAY 14: Storms 81
DAY 15: Tools 87
DAY 16: Birds 93
DAY 17: Revelations 99
DAY 18: Canada Thistle & Goldfinches 107

DAY 19: Meditation 113
DAY 20: The Seeds of February 119
Einstein.. 125
DAY 21: By Hand... 127
DAY 22: New Friends 133
DAY 23: Chaos and Order 139
DAY 24: Crickets 145
DAY 25: Bees and Lavender 151
DAY 26: A little every day 157
DAY 27: Baked Dirt 163
DAY 28: Experiments... 173
DAY 29: Currents 181
DAY 30: Seed Saving.. 187
DID YOU ENJOY THIS BOOK?................................ 191
GET YOUR BONUS 193
BOOK & GARDENING CLUBS................................ 195
ABOUT THE AUTHOR 197

INTRODUCTION*

I have always loved playing in the dirt - the tactile nature of it, sifting it through fingers, funneling it through cupped hands. It helps me think without dwelling. So, I guess in technical terms that might mean that it helps my brain synapses work effortlessly and smoothly without getting stuck at a crossroads.

Fast forward 40+ years, and I began gardening - and discovered SOIL, not dirt. By then I had developed into an artistic math nerd, lawyer, and research hound, and was embarking on homeschooling my daughter who wanted more butterflies to chase.

Most sane people would have simply bought a butterfly bush, maybe a little purple echinacea, and called it a day. Not me. I needed to fix my sloping backyard, find better sun exposure, and research "How to Grow Soil."

Ultimately, after the backyard butterfly project and a few community-garden raised beds with "Square Foot Gardening" (still my favorite book to recommend to new gardeners), I came to love growing soil more than growing tomatoes and cucumbers. Don't get me wrong - I still want the toms and cukes. But what really gets me psyched is learning new ways to make the earthworms happy and the soil tilth darker, looser, and more sweetly aromatic.

And in the average rich but compacted, root-and-rock-bound soil of NJ, it is a challenge that I love embracing and solving - albeit slowly.

Which gets us to the reason for this book. I am an extremely cerebral person (both in my professional career and my hobbies) - so much so that without the help of my exceptionally extroverted husband of 25+ years, I would probably also be an absolute introvert living in a log cabin in the hinterlands of North Dakota with a dog for company. Now thanks to him, I'm just a moderate introvert.

Gardening balances my excessive cerebral activities by - literally - grounding me.

I improve when I garden. I didn't realize this at first except that I somehow felt more energetic after digging and kneeling and struggling with the earth for 3 hours. Instead, I came to learn of its impact on me from my family and friends who kept telling me that I looked so much better and happier since I had been gardening.

INTRODUCTION*

It is not that I was unhappy. But one acquires a furrowed brow and constant serious expression simply from the action of endlessly thinking and reading and number-crunching. I enjoy those things. But gardening is not just enjoyable - it puts me in a State of Joy.

Perhaps the State of Joy can simply be attributed to the direct interaction with the electrical, chemical, and biological aspects of the earth. But I think it is more than that.

I was lacking Balance. Much like someone who is always on the road needs some immobile home time, or a performer needs some quiet time - I needed to exit the space between my two ears and spend time physically engaged with the earth, moving soil by hand, one inch at a time.

(That is not to say that I don't use my brain cells for gardening - I do. Just ask my husband how many hours of riveting earthworm research dialogue he has been subjected to.)

When I gardened, I grew. I had personal "aha moments." I saw analogies between gardening and life. Its challenges, learning opportunities, and routines. I started writing about it.

The Gardener's Spirit

I am not positive, but I think other gardeners might also experience this. My hope is that we can use the daily thoughts in this book as a launching point (and as much a source of humor as a math nerd/retired attorney can provide) to make notes about our own personal insights and transformations.

Wishing you many happy earthworms and gorgeous, sweet-smelling soil,
Theresa

*Full Disclosure (although I am retired from the Rolls of the NJ Bar for over a decade, terms like *Full Disclosure* may never fully leave my vocabulary, so I thank you in advance for your patience – notice though, that I did however manage to allow myself the horror of leaving a few prepositions dangling): I almost never read the Introduction to books. I occasionally read them after I have read the book and want to learn more about the author and/or subject matter. So, if you choose to skip this Introduction, I completely understand.

Aristotle

In all things of nature there is something of the marvelous.

The Gardener's Spirit

DAY 1: Optimism

It is but a mere few months since I ripped out the diseased cucumber plants - those which, in the Spring, I had arduously debated whether to direct sow or transplant, those for which I had finally remembered to stagger the plantings, those which I had hoped would provide the essential element for at least a dozen pints of our beloved refrigerator bread and butter pickles for my friends and family.

The planning of March and April. The drought of May resulting in an undeterred late June planting. The beauty of July as foot after foot of vines grew up the trellises quickly, and then effortlessly blossomed with little yellow flowers - followed by the appearance in the blink of an eye of a plethora of 3-inch-long gorgeous little Kirby babies. Only to be stifled by a leaf virus, or blight, or whatever name has been given to that particular source of evil that trampled my hopes for one of my favorite garden rewards.
Followed by the guilt of not having protected them from said evil, and the turmoil of attempting to find its source to prevent its future return.

And yet - and yet, I have already begun to dream of and to plan next year's crop. What explains this phenomenon?

When Russell Page referred to a garden as "an expression of faith," he must truly have known the disappointment of dashed hopes - as well as the faith that causes us to return to the garden mere months later, knowing that while all hopes will not be fulfilled, some happy surprises will surely appear, and the mere experience - regardless of the bounty or lack thereof - will evoke a song of praise.

As Eleanor Perenyi put it, "To garden is to let optimism get the better of judgment."

That math nerd, the prudent analyst, the prepared soldier in me cannot make sense of this optimism. And it is not only optimism - but perpetual optimism. And that lack of "sense" (or "judgment" as Perenyi puts it), is exactly what my soul needs - a relief from the expected, the linear, the logical.

And maybe it is this almost spiritual optimism connected with the earth itself that allows me to let go of the linear in favor of something greater - perhaps, dare we say, a true connection with Creation itself.

DAY 1: Optimism

I can find no other explanation for my willingness to intentionally abandon "the better of judgment" in favor of an activity that improves my being, than that it must be connected to the Divine in a paradoxical way - as is the case with most spiritual practices.

And yet this perpetual optimism is also not completely foolish. Rather, like the fool in a Shakespearean tragedy, there is a truth or a value in it. Our gardener's optimism is paired with Problem Solving.

What will I do next year to guard against this year's evil destruction? Is there something I did this year that caused it (possibly transferring a virus from one plant to another with contaminated fingers or scissors)? Is there something that I could have done differently this year - that I have yet to learn, or have read or heard but have forgotten about - to have prevented it? Have I committed the symptoms to memory or a notebook so that I can quickly spot the intruder if it raises its ugly head next year? If so, what can I do to limit or interrupt its damage?

And this is exactly what my inner problem-solver/learner lives for - research. But the truth is, my hope for a successful batch of Kirbys next year (so fast on the heels of this year's disaster) comes BEFORE my research has even BEGUN. There is a faith that I will find something - even a small bit of advice that

The Gardener's Spirit

will help or even solve the problem - that precedes my research.

But it starts with hope. And that hope is evidence of faith. And that hope is fueled by past experiences that remind me that some things will work, and some will not, and some I have control over, and some I do not. And that whole package of faith, hope and uneven, multi-causal only-partially-controllable results is in and of itself a spiritual experience for me - and one that can only happen when I am holding soil and seeds.

DAY 1: Optimism

Thoughts

The Gardener's Spirit

DAY 2: Notes

I am convinced that there should be an ignition lock for gardeners in the form of a small notebook. That is, if you do not immediately jot down a few notes about what you planted and where, as soon as you get in the car to leave the garden, then your car will not start.

Of course, we would need a backyard gardener's version too - maybe a garden gate lock?

We know the problem all too well. Modern gardeners have only to pause and look at their phones, never mind enter the house or drive to the next destination, to be distracted from making the several brief but important notes that will allow us to resume our garden work later.

The obvious shorthand reminders that we make in the garden to help us remember where we left off or what we planted where, seem obvious at the time. However, with the passing of a mere few hours and some phone calls, what once seemed obvious becomes incredibly vague.

The Gardener's Spirit

I experienced this first-hand the other day when planting garlic. My garlic gets planted 4 inches deep, plus a couple inches of mulch on top for good measure.

As the sun set, I needed a quick in-garden marker - usually a stick or row of rocks - to indicate where I left off in the ten-foot-long bed. That was easy, I will just put straw over the part that I planted and mulch over the part that I had yet to plant. I will remember. Of course, I will remember.

And I am driving straight home, right? I will enter it into my gardening notebook as soon as I get home.

Did I enter it into the notebook? Nope. My life is like yours - filled with texting, phone calls, a spouse, children, clients, work, housework, errands, a dog, neighbors, friends, projects, "to do" lists, music, news, and YouTube videos. That garlic planting note never stood a chance against those odds.

A few days later I was on my hands and knees staring at mulch to my left and straw to my right. Sure enough, I picked the wrong one. It was only after I had dug up 3 previously planted garlic cloves that I relented to the fact that I was in the wrong section.

DAY 2: Notes

It only took a few days for my brain cells to fail me and my logic to become reversed.

And it does not seem right nor just that I should need a paperwork or note-taking SYSTEM for gardening. I need them for work - but now gardening too?

Do I love making notes and plans and lists and charts in my gardening notebook in the Spring? Absolutely. But somewhere around the sweaty, humid, 90-degree days of July, when the planting is done and the daily pruning, weeding, mulching, watering, and squash-bug picking is in full swing, the habit of regular garden journaling gets tossed aside in favor of standing in front of the freezer to cool off.

I do not want to give up my garden journal with all the drawings, and planting schedule (that is always adjusted), and diligent notes about the locations of specific brands and varieties, and their germination dates, and the corresponding harvesting schedule. But I need something faster and less comprehensive when I am leaving the garden - before the rest of life takes over.

If not an ignition lock, then perhaps a small little pocket notebook on the dashboard might do.

The Gardener's Spirit

Of course, this is where non-perfectionists, non-law-school-trained, non-research-addicts have a huge advantage over me. This small little pocket notebook would require me to write brief, short notes - and then STOP.

I do not do well at trusting that a less-than-thorough note will be sufficiently helpful at a later date. Shouldn't I also add the list of the next 3 things to be done? And the six other observations that I made about other plants? And my idea for completely rearranging the garlic planting locations for the lower section of the garden? And how will I merge the notes from the little notebook into the larger "this full season" notebook?

At this point, I have choices - (a) write the short note of, "plant the next cloves in the mulched section of the former red leaf lettuce bed" and close the notebook and drive, or (b) attempt that, but allow my obsessiveness to take over and keep writing for 20 more minutes (thus ensuring that I am less likely to even open the notebook next time), or (c) just stare at the little notebook, shake my head at the ridiculousness of the mental dissonance, and put the car in drive.

Gardens show us our weak - or, non-existent - habits.

DAY 2: Notes

Gardens challenge us to grow out of our insane little behaviors - obsessiveness, worrying about merging notebooks as if I am preparing a Supreme Court brief, etc.

The Gardener's Spirit

～ *Thoughts* ～

_____

_____

_____

_____

_____

_____

_____

_____

DAY 3: Adaptation

Hang around with gardeners long enough and you will hear things like, "it takes seeds about 3 years in my garden to really adapt."

Before I gardened, I thought it was as simple as: you buy the seed, you plant the seed, you harvest the crop. Then, the following year you start over again by buying more seeds. It never occurred to me that there was the option of a fourth step. And I was clueless about the idea that the fourth step may have benefits not only to me, but to the plant as well.

As gardeners, we know that it is a beautiful rite of passage to move beyond the buy-plant-harvest process to the experience of seed saving.

And once we enter that theater of the life cycle, we begin to understand it on a deeper level. The plant from which we are now collecting seeds has just succeeded in a lengthy list of accomplishments:
- germinating - IN MY SOIL
- setting true leaves
- growing past the initial sprout stage
- setting flowers

- setting fruit
- growing fruit to maturity free of disease
- surviving attacks by insects and four-legged visitors

In that entire process, the plant has started the process of adaptation to my soil, my latitude's sun angles and intensity, my weather, my rocks, my air, my nutrients, my pests, my beneficial insects, and my water.

One year, I took my first stab at seed saving with cucumbers and tomatoes. But it was not until the following year when I stumbled upon the concept of adaptation. I was in shock that it had taken me so long to realize that the seed from the plant that had just grown in my garden would then be better able to thrive in my garden the next year than the "new" seed that I would purchase from ANY supplier the following spring.

How had I missed this? Of course the seeds gathered from cucumbers in California were going to behave differently in my soil than seeds from cukes that had adapted to the soil and weather in my particular corner of New Jersey.

DAY 3: Adaptation

This was a revelation far beyond the general climate guideline of, "Rhubarb doesn't grow in Mississippi, and Okra doesn't grow in Massachusetts."

And then I started hearing it repeated from experienced gardeners - "it takes about 3 years" - and started to truly appreciate what they were saying. There is a process going on. A process that I could not see, or touch, or influence - never mind control.

This opportunity to interact with garden processes that are beyond my control is one of the many therapeutic effects that the garden has on me. This particular one - benefiting from a process that is totally beyond my control - obviously helps to temper my need for control.

Nature and the earth were having a discussion with my seed-bearing plants that would only allow me to benefit from it - but not to influence it. The idea stunned me - that without a book, college lecture, or focus group - the seeds contained in this overgrown cucumber now contained a new, revised formula that would allow it to thrive in my garden soil and air next year even better than its parent plant had done this year.

I was the beneficiary. It was a pure gift. All I had to do was to collect the seeds.

The Gardener's Spirit

Which left the question, "What adaptations did I personally experience this year in the garden?"

Am I stronger, more resilient, more creative, or wiser in my interactions with the garden after 2 seasons with this specific garden? Am I a better steward of the soil, the space, or the seeds?

In general, I think I am. But, at the end of the season, it is always a challenge not to allow the season's "failures" to outshine fabulous "successes." Gardening is gently softening the hyper-critical side of me. While I still view things as failures versus successes, it is tempered by a simultaneous consideration of the several things that I learned from the experience - which often have a longer-lasting impact that far surpasses this current outcome.

I am definitely more connected with the ground. My legs have learned the steps of the almost hundred-foot length of the garden - its bumps, curves, slopes, and of course, rocks. I have come to accept - not yet embrace but at least accept - that nature has more of a say in what happens here than I would like, i.e., than I could ever control.

DAY 3: Adaptation

And the cure for lack of control is to adapt. So, in the acceptance of the reality that I have influence but not control over results, I am adapting to nature's way.

There is another adaptation that a long-term gardener makes - to become more of a custodian of the life in our care, rather than an umpire judging strikes and balls. On my best garden days, when I walk through the garden, talk to the cosmos through their long growth cycle, kneel and inspect the butternut squash flowers, nudge cucumber vines up a trellis, nod at the garter snake sneaking past, and gently prune the tomato plants, the more I experience it as a steward.

To be a steward of a garden means more than simply planting, watering, pruning, and harvesting.

It is the diligent and yet also emotional - even spiritual - experience of nurturing, protecting, encouraging, watching, listening, and attentively responding to one of the most essential aspects of creation - the fruition of the life of a seed.

How lucky we are when the garden uses its adaptation process to transform us from laborers into stewards.

The Gardener's Spirit

~~ Thoughts ~~

DAY 4: Coffee

It was not until I was able to move from a community garden of pre-made 4x8 raised beds to a wide open 2,000+ square foot section of a field that I felt the joy of walking through the garden with a cup of coffee.

When we leave the house, we often tell our families about our garden "to do" list for that day - planting seedlings, staking tomatoes, creating new beds, adding mulch, improving pathways - weeding! (or in my case, weed whacking)

But I could never actually start my "gardening" with anything but a complete walk through to check on my burgeoning "friends with roots." I mean, really, how could I just walk past the cosmos without brushing them with my fingers and whispering to them how tall and strong they are getting? And the cucumber seedlings have grown a foot and already have a few bright yellow flowers. Am I really going to skip the joy of kneeling and breathing in this wonder?

And coffee in hand makes this intoxicating routine about perfect. When the birds sing and butterflies sail past while you are walking through, well, then it is perfect.

In true paradoxical form, it is a perfect experience even though everything in the garden is not growing perfectly. The connection with not just nature - but with the very miracle of the entire growth cycle, with all its known and unknown intricacies - triggers an emotional state of simultaneous joy and contentment that is rarely found in other parts of our lives. Occasionally in music or art, or athletic competition, and certainly in raising a child. But rarely as part of a daily "routine."

In truth, it is as close as I can come to touching the Divine outside of prayer, raising a child, great art and music, or superior feats of athletics.

And "all" it takes is a little soil, sun, and seeds. Of course, that could not be farther from the truth. It takes work. But somehow, the labor (often sweaty, exhausting, muscle-aching labor in 90-degree days) makes the subsequent enjoyment greater. Sure, walking through someone else's garden is nice, even pleasant, and relaxing. But it is not necessarily joy-filled or spiritual.

DAY 4: Coffee

I do not think that it can be explained simply as, "I put my sweat into this, so I am getting more satisfaction in the rewards." It is more complex than that.

Our gardening labors engage us in the process of the Creation of a living thing. We are not the Creator - but we participate in the process. Each of us chooses how we want to participate. We use machines, or mechanical tools, or our hands and feet. There are as many styles of participating in Creation as there are unique souls.

For me, I find that the more I engage kinetically - with hands in the soil, nose in the flowers, eyes on the leaves, muscles moving rocks and soil - the more expansive and deeper is the joy that my soul experiences.

My ultimate gardening joy occurs when I am (1) digging in the dirt (or soil, depending on the spot) (without gloves) and (2) talking to my little Plant Kingdom friends. Truth be told, even while I am digging in the dirt, I am still talking, but with my other Creation colleagues - those without roots, i.e., the earthworms, and slugs, and my other non-microscopic soil-borne friends.

Any day that I am digging in the dirt and talking to my "friends with roots" is a good day.

The Gardener's Spirit

What is so ironic is that in my social/business life, I have a limited daily word allotment. Once I have reached that limit, I am not fit for human consumption and start to become incoherent.

But, talking to my "friends with roots," alone, with a cup of coffee, seems like one of the most natural things in the world to do. As natural as crunching numbers in my head (i.e., my math-nerd hobby).

Add the sun, and the breeze, and the birds and the bees, and I might never leave the coffee-walkthrough time - except that I have work to do to keep my "friends" thriving.

And so, with the empty cup set aside, I pick up the packet of seeds, the trowel, the cotton string, and the mulch, and proceed to the labor part of the experience.

DAY 4: Coffee

Thoughts

The Gardener's Spirit

DAY 5: Restored

I almost did not go to the garden. Honestly, why bother today? I had already put too many things on my schedule. I would only have an hour. How much could I get planted in one hour? Not much. I could go tomorrow.

I went. I was so happy that I did. I was happier when I left than when I arrived.

I was restored.

I know this. We all know this. And yet, the garden constantly surprises me with how much I am rejuvenated by merely being in its presence. Unlike so many other things in life, its value to me is not measured by the *amount* of productivity or accomplished tasks.

Rather, its value lies in its innate adjustment to my total being, an awakening of my spirit that no checkmarks on a To Do List could achieve.

And that is why, on this day, despite only having planted 20 little garlic cloves, I sang in the car ride home like a little kid, with the windows open on a chilly day, without any concern for the curious looks of the other drivers.

In full disclosure, I do not just arrive at the garden, hop out of the car with the seeds and spade in hand, and start digging. I walk through the garden. "Walk" is really a euphemism – I experience the plant, the growing spaces, the memories of the season's life, the ideas for the future life to come.

Regardless of the time of year, I reconnect with my "friends with roots." Or, in late Fall and Winter, with the spaces where those friends once stood, and have now transformed the soil for the next set of friends that will be planted there.

And I get excited all over again.

So, the garden, regardless of its current state, allows me to relive the joy that is, was, and will be. It transcends the moment. It enlarges my sense of gratitude for what is and was. It awakens hope for future adventures – and excitement for the blank canvas which is to be painted.

DAY 5: Restored

Thoughts

The Gardener's Spirit

DAY 6: Big Rocks

I broke a tine off my garden fork today. Why? Because I was impatient.

So, while I would like to blame the very large rock that was buried a foot below the surface of one of my soon-to-be tomato plants, the blame lies squarely with me – more specifically, with my inability to control my emotions at that moment.

I was tired, and probably hungry. But more importantly, I was thinking about all the things I was going to do as soon as I got this gosh-darn $%*@ rock. out. of. this. ground. (*snap*)

Simply put, my head had left the garden and was no longer where my feet were at. My head and my feet were not in the same place. That is always a bad formula for me. It encourages my worst self to show up.

Did I snipe at someone? Did I get upset over a little "spilled milk?" Did I misplace the notebook that I just had in my hand? Guaranteed I was thinking about some future "To Do List" item – or, more probably,

The Gardener's Spirit

about the six more things that I "needed" to add to the list, and worrying about how I was going to "get it all done."

And so, I stopped, bent down, and pulled the tine from the dirt (and at that spot in the ground, it was absolutely dirt, not soil). Then I stood, looked around to reorient myself, and took a deep breath.

My better-self appeared – I was standing in one of my favorite places, using muscles I usually neglect, doing work I love, bringing to life plans that I had drawn, and breathing fresh air.

At this point, I would have usually chastised myself for allowing myself to get impatient, or for my mind to wander to tasks of another place and time.

But I didn't. I reminded myself that I was here to enjoy this – every bit of it, mistakes and all – guilt-free. The kind and supportive side of me (the side that shows up for almost everyone except me) also reviewed my sanity tenets – that thinking of other things would sap all the joy out of gardening, would not accomplish striking things off my "To Do List," and would cause me more problems. And I "allowed" myself a break.

When I am in the garden, I am nicer to myself – which really means that I am saner, and thus, wiser.

DAY 6: Big Rocks

In the garden, my Sane-Self shows up to nurture me – instead of my Tyrant-Self to judge, criticize, push, keep score. How do I not only allow, but embrace, a tyrant of my mind when in real life I obviously abhor them?

Tyrants are very different than good motivators. Good motivational coaches use wisdom, struggle, structure, games, and flow, to draw out the best of you, not the worst. My inner tyrant is not a motivator. Once it appears, it relinquishes power only in the face of a complete meltdown that results in me looking (finally) to the Divine to help me escape from its claws.

So, I am very grateful to the garden for allowing me to practice sanity. The more sanity practice I get, I less often my inner tyrant shows up. I am still baffled by this cause and effect; it is poetical, not linear.

My gardening allowed me to quickly let go of the "error" that resulted in a broken tine, and even more, to fairly instantly learn from it – "Oh yeah, remember to keep your mind where your feet are at."

And so it came to be that a very big rock helped me practice treating myself well, and encouraged my saner self to show up more often.

The Gardener's Spirit

The next hour was a joy. Did I get on my hands and knees, with a small handheld rake (or claw, or cultivator, depending on your vicinity's nomenclature) and a spade? Absolutely. And I loved it.

DAY 6: Big Rocks

Thoughts

The Gardener's Spirit

DAY 7: Small Rocks

Stick a spade into any square inch of my garden soil and you will hear a thud. Also known as the spade finding a rock. Yep, any square inch.

Or at least that was the situation in the inaugural year of my garden.

In the fields of New Jersey, there is an endless supply of small rocks in the silver dollar range. And I had attempted to remove every single one that I encountered (along with any larger rocks).

After all, I thought, my tomato plants' roots would suffer when confronted with them. (Find me a New Jersey gardener whose gardening plans don't revolve around our beloved toms, and I'll show you a transplanted Southerner.)

Previously, other than the soil-growing experiments in my backyard, I had only gardened in the raised beds of local community gardens. Beautiful, loose topsoil to which I would add compost (from big box stores) and food for my worm friends (corn meal and oatmeal). There was not a stone larger than a half inch in sight.

So, of course, in Year 1 of this 2,000-square-foot garden carved out of farmland, I was concerned about the anticipated stagnation of my plants' roots by the multitude of rocks. Despair quickly followed. If I could barely dig a four-inch square hole for this one seedling, how would I ever accomplish the many "recommended" twelve-inch square ones that were needed for my flat of toms who were desperately awaiting a home?

Of course, can I learn about life like a normal person? Nope. Rocks are my teachers.

Here are two of my hard-fought lessons:

First, I found that, more often than not, when I thought I was wrestling with a BIG rock, I was actually dealing with a Tetris puzzle of small rocks. They had assembled themselves so expertly that they became an entity greater than the sum of its parts. I could not remove just one. And I could not remove it en masse. I had to find the strategic keystone that would unlock the entire Tetris building.

Then it occurred to me. Could I arrange MY SMALL ROCKS – my habits, pieces of my character, my

DAY 7: Small Rocks

emotions - so that they could provide me with a stalwart core to withstand life's challenges that well? Perhaps I could go one step farther. Maybe a dovetailing of my small habits and traits would give me the inner strength and courage to run headlong toward (and surmount) life's hurdles in pursuit of my goals.

Small habits, like small rocks, can be transformed into a strength greater than the sum of its parts.

Second, I found that these small, seemingly harmless rocks, seemed to be glued together. Superglued in fact.

Hours of video watching and blog- and book-reading later, I learned about the magic of the soil biology. When soil biology is cranking, the soil becomes aggregated – supple and aerated. The rocks remain. In fact, thanks to the new soil biology, they can now fulfill their purpose – to feed the toms.

But here is the real discovery – the solution to getting the soil biology cranking is MORE roots, not less. This boggled my brain. Here I am worried that my tomato seedling would have enough trouble getting its nutrients from this rock-filled soil/dirt. I would have viewed any additional plants as competition for those nutrients. But of course, my human logic was wrong. Miraculous nature has its own ways.

Paradoxically, the multiplicity of roots provides an abundance of biological activity that, (a) transforms dirt into soil, (b) aggregates the soil with plant exudates, thus creating air and water ways, and (c) erodes rocks, thus releasing its nutrients to the plants.

After paying a bit more attention to soil biology, low and behold I stuck my space into the soil, and voila it went down four inches, without hinderance – and despite there being rocks in the midst. Why? Because the soil's biology was in full swing and had created beautiful soil, which the rocks complimented.

And so, I came to learn that compacted soil is a wholly different matter than soil with lots of rocks.

Just as we are entirely different than a pile of bone and sinew. We were created to learn as well as to do. And we operate in a spiraling cycle, like nature – to apply our learning to the next level of doing, thus resulting in the opening of more upward paths to continued learning and contributions to society.

But to be effective, most of our learning comes in stages – what we are ready and able to hear, absorb, and apply at any given time. I was barely ready to

DAY 7: Small Rocks

understand how to get a seed to transform into a seedling, never mind simultaneously being conscious of the difference between dirt and soil, and certainly not its underlying biology. Even if I had been exposed to all that info at once, it would have been too many details to apply simultaneously.

I find that my character, personality and emotional development are similar. I could read 10 personal growth books in a month. But my ability to put apply all that info into daily operation the following month would be slim and none. The wisdom from those books needs to be considered, processed, aborded – and then applied – a bit at a time – if it is to be effective and lasting.

The Gardener's Spirit

~~~ *Thoughts* ~~~

DAY 8: Gloves

Every spring they call to me from the store displays: well-made, fresh, clean, colorful protectors of my fingernails and hands.

I promise myself that I will use them this year. I mean, why would I intentionally harm my fingernails (for which I am currently taking vitamin E to beautify them)? Or put dirt under them only to be removed later with 5 minutes of scrubbing?

But, knowing my history with gardening gloves, I put an inexpensive version into my cart – in the rare event that I diverge from my usual gloveless gardening.

The truth is that I absolutely love the feel of dirt – and soil. Wet, dry, loose, compacted. If it is of the earth, I am touching it – and without a glove on. There is a great photo of my 3-year-old self with my 2-year-old sister (the yin to my yang) that captures our core spirits – she is jumping to the sky, and my hands are in the dirt.

Are there times when I prefer gloves? Yep. For that Canada Thistle. Boy those puppies get yanked quickly and confidently with nice, thick gloves. But even at that, I have learned to dispatch them without gloves – I cut them at the base of the stem, and then using the scissors as tongs, relocate the soon-to-be-dead prickly greens to a nearby pile.

My therapist would probably say that the feel of the soil "grounds" me. It keeps me immersed in the present moment. The feel of the soil protects me from the ever-negative mental chatter of my "negative committees," the ones that want me to focus obsessively on my imperfections, fears and insecurities. It prevents my creative and intellectual pursuits from luring me into endless imaginations that don't have any real-life result – like the siren song of Harry Potter's mirror that makes wishing its own end.

When I am digging in the soil with my bare hands, up close, often on my hands and knees, usually talking to it, I feel the soil. I feel the soil, and it makes me feel. But it makes me feel – in a healthy, constructive way. And that is a miracle because feeling things is tricky for me.

I have loved intellectual pursuits from early on. Like math. At age 4.

I have also loved creativity from early on. Like age 6.

DAY 8: Gloves

But these two qualities meant that I spent a good deal of my life erroneously treating my emotions as (a) Non-Existent, or (b) Everything. (If you were to ask my family, they would probably suggest that a 26-volume book set might barely suffice for them to fully describe the "joys" of life with me during that time.)

The feel of the soil somehow allows my emotions to be accessible to me – and in a regulated way.

When my hands are in the soil, I do not lie to myself that life can be lived as an emotionless "perfectly" controlled experiment. Inversely, neither do I launch into overwhelmingly excessive emotions because of a $10 parking ticket (resulting from being 15 minutes late putting quarters into a meter). Well, at least most of the time. Okay, well, at least more of the time.

I am somewhat more of an integrated human being – both earthly and spiritual, with intellect, emotions, and relationships. And, having never experienced "integrated" before 50, I can honestly say that I love it so much that I am unwilling to go back.

And holding soil, moving soil, smelling to soil, unlocks that integration door for me.

So that probably means that, for the well-being of others, I should keep a pot of soil with me at all times for episodes of overly-controlling and excessively-emoting emergencies. (Maybe a brilliant entrepreneur will launch a product that serves this need, like the pet rock of the '70s.)

But fortunately, I find that the more I garden – specifically, the more I am holding soil – the more that emergency treatments are less necessary. (Although admittedly, it does get a little dicey during winter.)

DAY 8: Gloves

Thoughts

The Gardener's Spirit

DAY 9: T-shirts

I am fairly certain that I was absent the day that God was handing out the fashion gene. The person at the party wearing the plaid shirt with striped pants? Me. Or possibly I chose the mint green shirt to wear under the Kelly-green sweater. And these are the examples of when I worked hard at looking good. The harder I try, the worse it gets. Clothes simply baffle me.

Given my math-nerd spirit, this is not surprising. However, it does seem somewhat odd given that I am also an artist (okay, well maybe not exactly an artist, but a very creative person who can draw). So, you would think that I would have some color sense.

But, alas, not when it comes to clothes. All the choices confuse me. And yet, somehow, deciding which tomato varieties to grow this year, from amongst several catalog pages, is easy. Choosing the next step in a logic problem is a piece of cake. But what shirt to wear with what pants? It might as well be rocket science.

The Gardener's Spirit

(This is why my go-to business outfit is a blue long-sleeve collared button-down shirt or polo shirt with black slacks. It's simple. It works. Why confuse myself at the start of the day?)

Which brings us to the shocking truth that I get excited about selecting which T-shirt to wear that day to the garden. Surely my wires got crossed somewhere. Who has this sort of paradox running their life?

What is my mood today? The hot pink T-shirt that was on sale for $2.99 that is so bright that the cosmos might need to shield their eyes? The forest green T-shirt from one of my favorite YouTube farming channels? The light blue crew neck that fits loosely and won't stick to me in the mid-day heat?

The T-shirt has no rules – except what I feel about it that day. It needs only to match my mood – Goofy. Fun. Crazy. Creative. Determined. Heart-warming.

It is like being a kid again and feeling like the world – the day – is my oyster – there to offer me nothing but fun and adventure. Free-spirited. No guardrails. Any T-shirt I want. Destined – indeed intended – to get dirty.

DAY 9: T-shirts

So, I choose with reckless abandon. I need some reckless abandon in my life. And some serious order. (I would just like them to be appropriately matched with their objective.)

And so it is that choosing the day's T-shirt has become one of my many joys of gardening – just as choosing the day's coffee cup is. Isn't it funny how these little things add to our gardening experience?

How many of us have these quirky little accoutrements to our gardening addiction, I mean, activity?

Is it choosing your favorite gloves? Or the clippers for the day? Or which garden shoes to wear? Or maybe the perfect hat that matches your mood? Or is it the selection of basket, bag or container for today's harvest?

By embracing the whimsy of these fun daily choices, we elevate our own individual gardening experience. Perhaps in so doing, we can also feel our gardener's spirit skip between the rows.

Thoughts

DAY 10: Rain

Reflecting on rain in a gardening book is somewhat akin to commenting on colors in the fashion industry. It would take at least three volumes. So, as I use this brief space to spare us the 1,000 pages, please forgive my lack of thoroughness.

Let me admit right up front that I have never looked at the weather forecast so often in my life. Nor have I allowed it to have such an impact on my schedule.

In the spring (in New Jersey), my relationship to the weather forecast is somewhere between a puppy waiting for a treat and a pilot circling the airport waiting for the "cleared to land" message.

With an average rainfall of over 40 inches, we are blessed here with a good deal more rain than most of the country – and I am very grateful. The timing and nature of the rain, however, tends to occur exactly opposite of my gardening plans.

This leads me to think that we should start our own weather forecast app. I am fairly certain that our accuracy rates would be on par with or better than the professionals' predictions. Let us consider this for a moment:

Did we just plant 3 rows of seeds?
Tomorrow's Weather Forecast: 3 inches of pounding rain resulting in the creation of a "River of Seeds."

Did we just replant those 3 rows of seeds?
14-Day Weather Forecast: Unseasonably hot day-time temps – requiring almost daily watering to prevent seeds and seedlings from drying out.

Are the cherry tomatoes one day away from perfect picking?
Weather Forecast: 36 hours of consistent steady rain, ensuring that every single little jewel will s-p-l-i-t.

Are we booked solid with work and appointments for the next 3 critical planting days?
Weather Forecast: Beautiful, temperate sunshine with a light breeze.

We are aware that the rest of our neighbors also experience this paradox when their only available beach excursion opportunities are the weekends, which obviously coincide with the two rainy days each week. It is just that as gardeners, we are attempting to manage (and of course, by manage, I mean *control*) about 100 interconnecting activities.

DAY 10: Rain

But now, let us move past the subject of the rain's schedule and on to the consequences of wonderful rain – namely, mud. Truth be told, I thrive in the muddy spring garden. It gives me an opportunity to play, and in playing, to step into joy.

In the day-after-the-storm spring garden, messy is not only accepted but approved. In fact, I consider my muddy mud boots (aka muck boots) a badge of honor. Now, while I understand that gardeners of the slippery "Georgia clay" variety will probably feel differently than those of us up north, I love the feel of digging around in cool, wet mud.

As adults, how often do we have the chance to experience one of the favorite tactile activities of our young childhood? To mold, move, and meld MUD. I am not sure whether it is the activity or the substance itself that is so soothing. I suspect that it is for this very reason that spas can command large sums for mud baths.

And then there is the excitement of the challenge of working with – actually, mostly, working "in" – the mud to grow something beautiful and wonderful, to bring to life our sketches, our hopes. In those moments, I get as close to feeling sheer joy as I do when I listen to Handel's *Messiah's* Hallelujah

The Gardener's Spirit

Chorus. With as much humility as I can muster – I think we are created for just this purpose – to clumsily imitate the Divine act of creation. I know the customary *Genesis* account refers to being "from dust" but I suspect that "from mud" might be more accurate.

DAY 10: Rain

Thoughts

The Gardener's Spirit

Aristotle

Earthworms are the intestines of the soil.

Zig Ziglar

You can have everything you want in life if you will just help enough other people get what they want.

The Gardener's Spirit

DAY 11: Earthworms

Ask my husband to name my core tenet of gardening and he will say, "Feed the Worms." And he would be exactly right. He knows this because he has listened to me talk for hours about earthworms – what they do, how they do it, their varieties, their wintering habits, their eating habits, and their populations and activities on any given day in my garden.

Starting with the early days in my square-foot raised-bed gardening endeavors, the care and feeding of earthworms became my passion. I imported night crawlers from the local hardware store. I mixed cornmeal and rolled oats (in addition to compost) into my 64 cubic feet of top fill. I bought a leaf blower for the sole purpose of using the leaf shredder attachment to give the earthworms a mini-mulch below the wood mulch.

You have never truly experienced Mrs. Jones ogling you from behind her tomato cage until you pop open that 40-ounce canister of rolled oats. (Fortunately for me, the girls in my junior high were expert oglers, so I was unfazed.)

The Gardener's Spirit

I am convinced that earthworms are the key to good – and great – garden SOIL. The beautiful tilth and sweet earthy aroma that we dream of. Great garden soil can maintain an optimum temperature, release/retain water through torrents and droughts, bring nutrients to roots over 12 inches deep, and even help fight off blight and mildew.

And that brings us to the reason for the presence of Zig Ziglar, the renowned motivational speaker and sales trainer, in a gardening book.

Essentially, my gardening philosophy mirrors Zig's life philosophy:

> You can have everything you want in your garden if you will just help enough earthworms get what they want.

And by "everything," I mean the best chance for the best possible outcome given the circumstances that are beyond our control. Earthworms won't prevent the 40-mph windstorm. But they will give the roots the best chance of being strong enough to recover from it.

I suspect that my affinity for feeding earthworms is not unique among this audience. The more that I learn about soil – its incredible biological activity and

DAY 11: Earthworms

its intricate, almost paradoxical, plant-feeding operations – the more I grow convinced that earthworms are the heart of the garden.

In my new NON-raised 2,000 square-foot garden, earthworms become that much more critical to good soil. I have witnessed the results of their hard work over the past two years. They have transformed the super dense dirt, filled with a plethora of little and sometimes big rocks glued together, into soil – at least a couple of inches of soil anyway.

And that is why on any given day, you can see me on my hands and knees talking to – what appears to be – the ground. But in fact, I am talking to my friends, the earthworms. I apologize to them for disrupting them as I dig a hole for the transplants. I warn them to get out of the way, so I do not inadvertently harm them. I reassure them that their relocation while I plant is only temporary. I thank them for their hard work. And of course, I count them. (How could I not? I am a math nerd after all.) The last count of six within four cubic inches significantly surpasses last year's inaugural count of three within one cubic foot.

Earthworms make me a better person because they humble me. I cannot do what they do. At all. Even a little. And so, I am reminded daily in my garden that I cannot exist as a totally independent, self-sufficient,

The Gardener's Spirit

invulnerable island. I must depend on others. Both the human kind and the earthworm kind. And the more I garden, the more comfortable I get with that idea. In fact, I sometimes catch myself not just being resigned to the fact but rejoicing in it.

DAY 11: Earthworms

Thoughts

The Gardener's Spirit

DAY 12: Grasshoppers

On August nights, outside our bedroom window, cicadas serenade us as we read. Cicadas, but not grasshoppers.

As for grasshoppers, I have never had much interaction with them - until this year's garden when I discovered their unique personality.

I attributed their noticeable presence to my strolling through the continuing bunches of weeds, grasses and brush scattered among my veggies and flowers. But then I read some YouTube comments which referred to their higher than usual populations this year. (I am aware that some of us place them squarely in the "pest" category.)

Nonetheless, I find their company both amusing and comforting.

They invite me in. They hop ahead of me (not behind). Almost leading the way. And they sit and wait for me to catch up before hopping again.

The Gardener's Spirit

And they look toward me (not away). As if they have something to tell me about the garden events that I missed earlier in the day.

And so, I bend down and get to eye-level with them – and ask.

The one-sided chat consists mostly of questions like, "what happened," "what did you see," and "what do you know?"

And now you know my secret – I have an inner Doctor Doolittle who likes to talk to grasshoppers and earthworms. Umm, and bees. Oh, and ladybugs. (Okay, I'll stop now. I assume you've drawn the accurate conclusion that I am sometimes more comfortable with my garden friends than at a party, and I can now move on, fully embarrassed.)

I do not talk to the butterflies though. They have an air of majesty about them that causes me to give them a wide berth without disturbing them.

And so, the garden – or more accurately, my involvement in the garden – evokes a childlike wonderment in me. The child that imagines, creates, explores, and adores. Freely. Without care except for what is right in front of my nose, literally.

DAY 12: Grasshoppers

Am I always in that state of inspired engagement in the garden? No, not always. Not when my shirt is drenched from the summer heat, or when I am chastising myself for the delay in transplanting the seedlings. Not always. But often.

Mostly that wonderment bubbles up while I make my initial and departing strolls through the garden. It shows up when I show up. That is, when my head and heart are where my feet are.

If we are lucky, we have incorporated that childlike awe into our adult life in spaces and activities that so fully engage us that we operate in a bubble where time and judgment are suspended.

If we are extremely fortunate, we have someone in our lives to share those moments with. And so it is, that my husband is willing to watch me become animated about today's gardening adventures with grasshoppers.

He is wise enough to know that he is not merely listening to a story. Rather, he is witnessing me revisit my connection with the world in a way that brought out my most creative, imaginative, and joyful self:

> That childlike self, with the wisdom of adulthood, but also with the capacity to

believe without proof, who can look into the steady staring eye of a grasshopper and almost – almost – see the Divine spark that brought the world into being.

And when any of us give a loving witness to another's awe-filled experience, it multiplies the joy in both of us.

DAY 12: Grasshoppers

Thoughts

The Gardener's Spirit

DAY 13: Mystery

They should write gardening journals more like mystery books. Most gardening journals have a "data-entry" format, e.g., "Today I did this, this, and that."

But gardeners know that so much more of our energy is spent on trying to figure out "Who done it?" Most of our resources to solve our garden problems center around a list of pests and ailments (suspects), and on how to effectuate the "sentence" against a culprit.

However, this approach is onerous and confusing. I mean, does Poirot look at an alphabetical list of suspects and start guessing "Who done it?" Does he start his path to determining the culprit by learning about the criminal's preferred targets and methods? No! He starts with the body, his observations and interviews.

So, why are we burdened with memorizing 200 pages of all the victims and the methods of a plethora of suspects to determine "Who done it?" It seems rather backwards. Surely Sherlock would never tolerate such inefficiency.

Therefore (and, dare I say, obviously), we need a set of Detective Books (ideally with Holmes, Poirot and/or Marple) that solve gardening mysteries. As in, "The Mysterious Case of the Wilting Watermelon Leaves."

It would start with the problem (the wilting watermelon leaves) and work its way to the culprit (the xyz leaf virus). Chapter 1: The Gardener discovers the wilted leaves (cue screams of shock and horror). Chapter 2: Enter the Brilliant Detective, who dispassionately examines the victim and begins the forensic assessment. Chapters 3 to 5: Our Detective asks the Gardener a series of probing questions that reveal relevant facts and observations – or lack thereof. The Detective uses that info to narrow down the list of suspects. He then further compares that gathered evidence against the plant's and the suspects' eccentricities.

Chapter 6: And then the little gray cells ponder. Chapter 7: And voila! We correctly identify the culprit, and (Chapter 8) adjudicate the method of dispensing with the little devil.

Wouldn't this be so much more effective than our current method of: find a problem, scream, guess, research everything, attempt a solution, re-read everything we read last year, guess, attempt a different solution, repeat?

DAY 13: Mystery

Not to mention, more fun!

I love the detective aspect of gardening. Gardening provides me with one of life's most prolific problem-solving adventures.

Some people are unaware that the combination of creativity and logic can create a problem-solving addict. (In fact, I am often justly accused of jumping in with a "solution" when my friends are simply trying to share their feelings with me.)

Why be satisfied with a mere crossword puzzle or logic problem when you could have hundreds of square feet each creating its own multitude of problems in one growing season? (And all without an "Answers" section at the back of the book.)

The trick for me is to remember that each gardening "Who Done It?" is a problem-solving opportunity, rather than a test that I ace or fail. (Ask me how inept I am at dealing with failure in a rational way.)

And of course, the more problem-solving that I do in the garden, the more I apply that approach to life's daily challenges – rather than taking the very narrow pass/fail view that results in sapping my joy, rather than adding to it.

Thoughts

DAY 14: Storms

I love storms. The winds howling. The sky delivering its deluge. The snow, sleet and hail pelting the ground. The lightning heralding the arrival of the pounding thunder.

Storms invigorate me. At the same time, they prompt me to hunker down and create a protective enclave from the quasi-danger. They create a paradox, which is probably why I love them – because my life is filled with paradox.

While my geography gets neither tornadoes nor Cat 5 hurricanes, we are visited by some serious storms during gardening season.

The torrential rains come in the spring. The thunder and lightning prevail in mid-summer. Tropical storms arrive in September. And hail, well, hail threatens us in every season.

What does this mean as a gardener? It means that the weather's massive systems override the issues of soil, disease and pestilence, i.e., those issues over which I have some influence if not control. It means I have absolutely zero control.

Intellectually I know that there is nothing I can do to stop the 4 inches of rain from washing away a week's worth of planting seeds. Also, I must watch the hail bouncing off my deck while knowing that my green bean seedlings will be irrevocably destroyed. And finally, as I listen to my weather-band radio during the power-outage, I know that the tomatoes, along with their stakes, will be lying on the ground when I next see them.

Eventually I get to a place of resignation, but not before going through the anguish of not being able to protect my wards.

So, as a gardener, an internal process occurs with every serious storm:

1. My storm-generated excitement is dampened by my concern/worry over the garden.
2. I confront my inability to control all circumstances.
3. I resign myself to the reality that the best I can do is not always enough to protect my plants from harm.

DAY 14: Storms

A lot of expletives usually arise as I work my way from Step 1 and Step 3. And for me, it is work – to let go and to accept.

Sometimes an intense storm can make this acceptance easier than just an average summer rain. While my mind would normally have taken several trips around the analyzing mountain called "what could I have done better," it abandons that option now in the face of such severe weather. There is so little that I can do to protect my garden from serious flooding, hail, or tropical storm winds. So, the relinquishment of my will to the omnipotent weather has a high likelihood of occurring before sunrise.

My goal is to enter the post-storm garden expecting damage, hoping for the salvation of some plants, and open to the challenge of rebuilding and restoring.

I am fairly certain that this posture is the essence of every self-help book, yoga class, therapy session, and spiritual reading that I have ever read: expect life to be imperfect, do your best, realize you can't control everything, hope for the best, plan for the worst, and accept the challenge of improving what's right in front of you.

And so it is that gardening for me is actually a spiritual lifeline that keeps me grounded, centered –

The Gardener's Spirit

sane in fact. Its kinetic nature changes me and aligns me in a way that mere reading and intellectual thought cannot achieve.

Much like the storm's paradox, gardening presents me with a paradox that I often return to – that while my brain enjoys the theoretical garden-problem-solving work, my spiritual transformation occurs by my doing the physical gardening work.

DAY 14: Storms

Thoughts

The Gardener's Spirit

DAY 15: Tools

From April to November, my car is a tool shed. At first, I didn't know whether to be embarrassed by this, or proud.

I live in the country (having moved here from Manhattan over 20 years ago) – not totally rural, but beyond the suburbs. We have cows, sheep, bears, deer, foxes, rabbits and turkeys. We define traffic as more than two cars at the traffic light.

So basically, over 50 percent of my county's adult population drive pickup trucks. I really like pickup trucks. But I prefer an all-purpose vehicle. Thus, I have an awesome 4-door sedan. And, during gardening season, it serves as my pickup truck.

Like all hobbies, there is an endless supply of tools and accessories to assist us in our gardening. Each year I acquire a couple new items. So, this year's back seat inventory included: a shovel, a hoe, two types of garden forks, pruning shears, and an electric weed-trimmer.

The Gardener's Spirit

(That was in addition to the variety of garden supplements such as mulch, compost, newspapers, large pots and boxes, soil amendments, t-posts, and, on any given day, seedlings. I did fit two bales of hay in it – for the potatoes. That was also in addition to the trunk's contents of various cutting utensils, string, hand tools, old socks, aluminum foil, storage bags, yard stick, plant food, oatmeal, Epsom salt, bug spray, cleansers, paper towels, rags, wet-wipes, extra hats, knee cushions, sunscreen, etc. The seeds get to ride up front with me.)

From time to time, some concerned person approaches my husband with, "Have you seen Tree's car?" He just smiles, nods knowingly, and replies, "Yeah, she gardens."

Eventually, rather than being either embarrassed or proud, I came to consider my car-turned-pickup-truck to be an effective use of my time and assets, and an excellent conversation-starter. In short, a win-win.

While others may be spending their time and energy judging my car's backseat contents, I am spending mine happily growing tomatoes and feeding the worms.

My gardening tools are my problem-solving partners. Together we tackle big rocks and small. We attempt to

DAY 15: Tools

pound t-posts into rocky soil. We fight the good fight against the ever-pervasive Canada thistle. We are a team. Where I go, they go. At least most of the time.

There are those times when I need to pick up family members from the airport. This means adding 30 minutes to relocate the teammates to the garage. And if an empty trunk is needed for luggage, then that's an additional 30 minutes.

This does not discourage me though from contemplating what new tool or accessory will be my "top draft-pick" for next season. I am seriously considering a post-driver. My 6- to 8-foot tomato stakes (usually t-posts) are either leaning sideways because the soil is too loose or are barely two inches deep because it can't get past the rocks.

Alternatively, I could take the digging bar approach. I had never even heard of or seen this tool until I came across it in a YouTube video. Perhaps I should start a Gardening Wish List for birthday, Christmas and anniversary gifts. I mean, doesn't everyone ask for a digging bar for Christmas? This is where my grandson leans over and tells his mom, "You just never know with Grandma." (If Santa brought you a digging bar for Christmas, let me know how much grief you did or did not get from your family.)

The Gardener's Spirit

Regardless of your garden's location, or your mode of transporting your tools, you know that good tools help you make the magic happen. What tools are on your Garden Wish List this year?

DAY 15: Tools

Thoughts

The Gardener's Spirit

DAY 16: Birds

I am constantly listening to something while I do other things (like driving, working, or cooking). An audiobook (of fiction or non-fiction), a movie or tv show, YouTube (of how-to and/or entertainment), the business news, music of any given decade or genre. (On occasion, I do listen to a living breathing person.)

Most of the time, when I am in the garden, I listen to the high-energy rock and roll classics of the Billy Joel, AC/DC, and Queen variety on earbuds. It keeps me moving and digging. It keeps out the thoughts about the work and home "to do" lists. It keeps me "in the zone."

But, upon my arrival at, and just before my departure from the garden, I stroll through my garden. Without earbuds. Without music or audiobooks. Just me, talking to my friends with roots, and our other garden companions. And occasionally, the birds will swoop by with their songs.

They startle me every time. It seems silly to be thrown off-balance by birds when you are standing in the middle of acres of land in a rural setting. Of course I

The Gardener's Spirit

should expect them. And I love watching them at home, from my kitchen, while they visit the bird feeders on my deck. But when I am outdoors, fully engulfed in the garden, they surprise me – the way someone's voice would when you are entranced by a painting.

Their unexpected appearance jars me out of a state of total engagement with the earth-bound garden life (which of course, are mostly silent). The birds remind me that there are forces outside of my bubble.

And not any wimpy forces either, but powerful, dynamic, beautiful, even predatory, forces.

Finches and nuthatches, sparrows and wrens. Each with their own song. And occasionally a mockingbird, singing his unique medley of cover songs.

They announce their presence not only aurally, but kinetically – swooping overhead to a nearby fence post or chasing each other in a 3-D game of tag above the garden. Their motion brings a distinct shift to the garden's atmosphere, different from the wind, rain, or hopping frogs.

The electricity changes. And I catch my breath. And despite their interruption of my bubble, I am prevented from interacting with them. Their speedy

DAY 16: Birds

missions do not include me. Even when they perch nearby, they are too skittish to tolerate my attention, never mind my approach.

So, they have relegated me to the role of a mere mortal observer – a recipient, if you will, of their beauty and music. They remind me that they – unlike my plants – are beyond even my influence (as well as my control). In short, while I am standing there stunned, in awe of their graceful flight and incredible songs, they humble me.

And then, in that state of awe and humility, I remember what they eat. And my heart drops. My worms are at risk. I want to warn them, "Take cover! Periscope down! Dive, dive!" But Nature has her own balancing act, her own warning systems, her own life circles and cycles. And I must accept them as part of the terms of my gardening contract with her. (However, she does tend to haphazardly change the terms on her whim. No offense. Just sayin'.)

And then there are my friends, the Canadian geese. For some reason, they never startle me. Instead, the sound and sight of them always invigorate me.

Far from the startling songs of their smaller compadres, the honks of the geese sound more like CB-radio transmissions to me:

The Gardener's Spirit

"Breaker, breaker 1-9. Winter arriving in two – repeat – two weeks. Commencing southbound flights."

Of course, I look up – once again amazed at the organizational and communication systems of the entire Canadian geese population. And, as I would to friends departing for vacation, I reply,

"10-4 good buddy. V-formation looks good from here. Catch you on the flip-flop. Over and out."

The beauty of the geese experience is that there are multiple flights every season. Once they start in the Fall, you can expect them almost daily. The same holds true in early Spring. So, there is an expectation, a repeated ritual.

In the Fall, their honks, with their affirmation that cold weather looms around the corner, spur me on to step up my pace of my harvesting, winter planting and clean-up.

In March, their honks confirm my hopes – that Spring is almost here, despite the blustery winds and lingering snow. With the enthusiasm of a child, I wave my arms high in the air to welcome them back. And I am totally comfortable doing so, because, in my

DAY 16: Birds

garden, the geese and the flowers don't need me to act like a proper grown-up.

The Gardener's Spirit

～⌒～ *Thoughts* ～⌒～

DAY 17: Revelations

Spring weeds took over my garden this year. I write this as if they took aggressive action against my wishes, which in fact, is less than completely truthful. To be totally honest, I allowed them to do it.

As many successful corporate leaders know, when a problem arises, you can often find its true cause by looking back, way back, in fact several steps before the supposedly immediate triggering event. It is known as the "ask why five times" approach to problem-solving. And as many gardeners and farmers know, the same holds true in the garden and on the farm.

And so, at the beginning of April, I had to confront my activities of the previous October, November and December.

The first part of my fall prep had been to plant my first-ever garlic cloves. Some went into already-made beds. Some were dug into compacted soil that had not been used as a bed that season. Suffice it to say that in December, I was still planting garlic.

The next element of my fall prep had been to reconfigure the entire garden. That growing season had added 600 square feet to the garden, which had become five new huge 10' by 10' patches created by expanses of newspaper for mulch and weed suppression, held down by rocks, to grow watermelon, pumpkins, and butternut squash.

Now wanting to "rotate" crops, I wanted to turn those huge patches of hard, lifeless squares into workable beds. Of course, in my mind, the shredded leaves topped with manure and mulch were a given. Additionally, with my recent research into the elements of good soil, I knew that I wanted to keep living roots in the soil as long as possible (cover crops) and to do significant and extensive intercropping the following season.

Out came the drawing pad and colored pencils, and a significant redesign of the 2,000 square feet. It considered the garden world's lists of "friends" and "enemies." The onions could not be intercropped with the beans, etc. It contained winter cover crop strategies. It also FINALLY took into consideration the extremely uneven nature of the ground – its bumps, dips, twists and turns – and the random rock piles that I had formed while planting.

DAY 17: Revelations

It would guide the winter prep and transformation of the entire space.

Well, it would have guided it if I had had 50 hours a week and endless energy and resources to create the perfect 2,000 square feet of breathtaking spring beauty and organization.

Hey, I can dream. And I worked hard toward the dream. And then, as the garden is fond of reminding me, I deal with the reality of my limitations.

My rookie-year of planting cover crops started in November, in what had become an extended fall and very mild winter. I had created several different mixes of cover crops, many unorthodox. I experimented with them around the garden territory, with dreams of the springtime joys of observations, note-taking, and improvements. But as I was planting into newly unearthed, hard compacted soil, what was to become the site of next year's new beds, nature reminded me that cool colorful sketches are a starting point, not a magic wand.

And so, I learned that if your cover crops have not sprouted before the below-freezing temps and harsh winds arrive, then your future "beds" are left with no ground cover – no plants, no mulch, no compost, no newspaper, no cardboard. Nada, nothing, zilch.

The Gardener's Spirit

Do you know what future beds without winter ground cover are called? Weed plots.

And so, it came to be that in April I was not in fact making notes of my #1-10 cover crop mix experiments but rather, was confronted with the beginnings of weed plots. In response to which, I quickly formulated a master plan to clear them in patches, one little four-foot-square section at a time, as I did my planting. And since it was April, and my area's trusted planting date is Mother's Day for hardier plants, and Memorial Day for favorites like toms and cukes, I "had time." I also used that time to cart more mulch and compost into the garden.

Additionally, my weed-clearing was somewhat limited by my 1-hour capacity electric weed-whacker (I am embarrassed to admit that I am intimidated by gasoline-powered engines, which makes me feel like a wimp – yet one more humbling lesson of the garden).

I chose to use the situation as an experiment. I thought that if I left the living weed roots in the ground until I got to that section to create that "bed," then the soil would be better. This did in fact turn out to be true.

DAY 17: Revelations

However, I did not anticipate how quickly the weeds would grow strong and tall.

Over the winter, my research uncovered a lot of recent discoveries in the farming/gardening world. One being that the soil biology accounts for stronger, better growth than the previous theories centered around soil nutrients for improving growth and health.

Thus, having a living root in the ground keeps the soil biology active, and does more to create biologically active, loamy soil than just covering the ground with leaves and mulch. Not that they are mutually exclusive. More like, having the ground cover allows the living roots to last longer, do more work, be protected from the harsh cold and wind of the winter months, and be ready to have the living roots do their work quickly and extensively in the spring.

And therein lay my dilemma. Having left the garden mostly uncovered over the winter, except for some haphazard newspaper and cover crop seeds that never sprouted (until the spring), the spring garden was bare, raw, gray, and compacted. Void of both carbon matter and a cover crop.

Shipping in a truckload of compost and/or mulch was not an option. So, this year became the "let's let the weeds do the work of protecting and preparing the soil."

And it is working – for the most part. The less-than-ideal part is that, before I could plant the entire 2,000 square foot space, the weeds had grown more powerful than the weed-whacker. As of July, one large section remains. That section may become this winter's experiment.

I learned a few things from this experiment:

1. Bare soil that will not even grow weeds is problem soil. It is hard, compacted, and wormless.
2. Earthworms love weed roots. And weed roots love to wedge themselves between rocks. And those rocks get smaller and looser.

In the areas where a DIVERSE set of weeds grew, the soil was BEAUTIFUL. It was soft, darker than usual, alive with earthworms and arthropods, and filled with easy-to-remove rocks.

As to the roots of these hardworking weeds, they were expansive and deep, and contained lots of branches covered with "hairs."

DAY 17: Revelations

University scientists have discovered that those hairs are not actually "roots," but rather, the result of the plants absorbing and expelling bacteria – without destroying them. The more hairs, the more biologically active and better the soil.

And then it occurred to me . . . I was using the weeds as my "cover crop."

Thoughts

DAY 18: Canada Thistle & Goldfinches

I arrived at the garden having decided that my first priority (because, let's be honest, no gardener has just ONE priority per visit) was to cut down the five-foot-tall Canada thistle patch that I had allowed to fully flower and turn to seed. By doing so, I would allow more air circulation and sunlight onto the nearby tomatoes, flowers, leeks and thyme. It would also create more square footage for the fall crops and would give the soil time to dissipate the allelopathic chemicals before their planting.

If you are unfamiliar with Canada thistle, consider yourself lucky. It is an extremely invasive weed, spread by both underground runners and prolific seedheads. I think Canada might have declared it Enemy #1.

Why had I allowed it to grow? Because I wanted to see what would happen.

I knew from last year that it would regrow endlessly. So, I figured, why not let the existing plants grow to maturity instead of having twice as many plants sprout in their place? And I wanted to see what the flowers looked like. I wanted to see if my research was somewhat accurate, that is, that the weed's purpose was to indicate an alkaline soil and to bring calcium up from the depths.

So, I pull up to the garden, having enjoyed the thistle forest experiment, armed with sharp scissors – which, by the way, I have learned to wield masterfully. The trick is to cut the stem near the ground and then grab the thick stalk firmly with the scissors, using it as a set of tongs, without cutting it, and then toss it to the side, creating a pile of the thorny beasts. This completely avoids the need for gloves.

I personally do not have claustrophobia, but my hands might feel differently. They tend to rebel when I wear gloves. But that is topic for another day.

As a stand and look toward my objective, a brilliant goldfinch swoops in and lands on a tall Canada thistle, which bends slightly under its weight. I freeze, in awe.

Nature screams through my conscience, "The birds need the thistle."

In case you have never seen Canada thistle after it blooms its alien-looking pink and purple flowers,

DAY 18: Canada Thistle & Goldfinches

imagine dandelion powder puff globes, the kind we would make a wish on as kids, before blowing the seeds everywhere – only much bigger.

And I look on as this striking three inches of yellow animated aviary life shines through a tall mass of marshmallow-topped greenery.

Does he just like the view? Or does the view serve a survival purpose, like finding food?

Does he find it a convenient place to pause while swooping through the endless fields? Or does the thistle provide the perfect height and cover to escape his predators?

Does he use the thistle as an ideal place to communicate with his friends in the flock?

Does he want the fluffy tufts for his nests?

Anyone watching me standing motionless observing the spectacle and contemplating its meaning, would have been wondering when the heck I was going to get to work planting, weeding and watering.

Of course, being the avid – no, not avid, that's too tame, obsessive would be more accurate – researcher that I am, I looked up goldfinches. I can assure you that I was not prepared for my findings.

In fact, the goldfinch's genus name is Caruelis, which is derived from the Latin word carduus, which means – yep, "THISTLE." And of course, you guessed it, goldfinches depend heavily on thistle for food and do in fact use the "thistledown" in their nests.

Obviously, the thistles are still there. The goldfinch has attracted a couple of his friends to join him in the undulating swooping and thistle hopping. They are adorable to watch. They are like the teddy bears of the bird world – adorable bundles of happiness. If Winnie-the-Pooh was a bird, he would be a goldfinch.

So, the garden will now contain a perennial Canada thistle patch (don't tell the Canadian authorities), to keep the goldfinches happy and thriving.

Does that mean fewer tomatoes? Probably. But the happiness I get from keeping the goldfinches happy and fed surpasses even the best tomato and mayo sandwich.

DAY 18: Canada Thistle & Goldfinches

Thoughts

The Gardener's Spirit

DAY 19: Meditation

I hate meditating. Which means of course, that I am in desperate need of it.

My husband has been trying to get me to meditate for years. Sometimes he tries to sneak it into my life in the same way he would hide vegetables in my meals. "Hey, let's do just a short 5-minute walking meditation while we walk on the Appalachian Trail."

Like the old days of vegetable smuggling, I go along less than half-heartedly. Of course, afterwards, he feels refreshed and restored. I feel exhausted from spending 5 minutes telling myself not to think.

Yes, I am the Meditation-Challenged.

Enter gardening.

In the early spring, my Zone 6 gardening mainly consists of building infrastructure. Mostly, that means clearing weeds, digging up rocks, lugging compost, gathering leaves to make compost, etc. When doing a lot of this type of physical labor, I like to wear headphones and listen to the high energy three-chord rock of my youth. Sammy Hagar's "I Can't Drive 55," and its compatriots keep me moving without tiring.

But as spring slides into June, when my hands are more often playing in the soil, I prefer the soundtrack of the garden. The bees, the swishing weeds, the birds, the nearby goats and chickens, the wind, the cicadas.

And so, it was on a hot day in July, while I was on my hands and knees with the hum of nature filling my senses, digging up garlic bulbs one by one with my spade, that I found myself thinking of, well, nothing.

And then I realized, this is what my husband experiences when he meditates! It was awesome. And peaceful. And inspiring.

It was *The Zone*.

Later I began to appreciate that the garden gives me a significant amount of "non-thinking" Zone time. Gardening allows my brain to rest. And it definitely needs rest (*see* the first paragraph of this chapter).

I am a thinking being. I think about everything, all the time. You know the type. You might be the type. Of course, there is usually a good amount of doing happening simultaneously. But at any given moment, if you ask me what I am thinking, I will need to choose

DAY 19: Meditation

between several ideas, problems, analyses and solutions in constant motion in my mental jungle gym in order to answer your question.

So, you can understand my surprise at finding myself alive, breathing and yet, somehow, without force or intention, thinking of nothing. I had found my meditation portal.

Actually, I had not found it so much as realized that this had been occurring over the years when playing in the soil, but I had never noticed. What I HAD noticed was that I was happier when I left the garden. I was more grounded and more centered. Calmer. Clearer.

In case you are wondering, those around me were also enjoying life more. Perhaps not a mere coincidence.

Come to find out, I AM capable of clearing my mind, calming my nervous system, and tapping into a spiritual state. I just need, well, dirt.

And rocks. And roots. And earthworms.

I am hoping that other gardeners experience this. If so, it would make me feel less weird. It might also explain, at least in part, why so many of us return to the unpredictable, ever-challenging art, science and work of gardening.

This meditation portal has now become so important to my well-being that I am exploring different options to stay connected to the soil during the winter.

Some might suggest growing indoor plants. However, that activity does not put me in The Zone. In fact, it does just the opposite. I simply do not speak the language of indoor plants. Then I kill them, inadvertently, but inevitably. It might be the lack of earthworms. Or rocks.

So, this winter, if you happen to see me with a pickaxe trying to plant impatiens seeds into frozen ground, or laying on the ground in a parka talking to my winter rye cover crop, you'll know why.

P.S. For the record, I did consider deleting the "Thoughts" section in this chapter for obvious reasons. But I wasn't sitting in the dirt when I typed this, so my rule-following, logical side won out. You, on the other hand, are free to stay in *The Zone* and skip it.

DAY 19: Meditation

Thoughts

The Gardener's Spirit

DAY 20: The Seeds of February

Perhaps no topic (other than earthworms) engages my gardener's spirit more than seeds.

The spark alights in February. In a home surrounded by two feet of snow, snuggled on a cozy couch, I begin the "ooooo"-ing and "ahhhhh"-ing over catalogs filled with stunning images of summer vegetables and flowers. These could all be mine for the low, low price of . . .

It is not quite that I have mixed emotions. More accurately, I have a whirlpool of emotions which gather energy from each other and create an irrational spiral of optimism and recklessness.

Curiosity. I had no idea there were 8,239 varieties of tomatoes. Which hybrids are resistant to the evilness that attacked mine last season? Do they have the specific type of rhubarb that I couldn't find last year?

Recall. That YouTube gardener said that kale variety had better flavor. That article recommended bush beans for big-batch harvesting. That video used home-grown jalapenos to can Cowboy Candy.

The Gardener's Spirit

Imagination. That would be fabulous in soup recipes. I could have early spring color with those flowers. The family would love fire-roasted salsa with five types of tomatoes.

Inspiration. I wonder if I could grow that? We've never had home-grown potatoes before. I could build a whole new bed just for them.

Determination. This is the year that I start my own herbs from seed.

Annnnd that's when I know that I have gone over the edge.

I sigh, and force myself to stand up, hide the catalogs in a dark corner of a bookcase, step outside and breathe in the 10-degree air to recover from my stupor. I mean really, how can I fit one more variety of tomatoes, a new butterfly bush, three more types of herbs, a third type of cucumber, and two entirely new vegetables into my already overcrowded garden? Of course, I could discontinue or replace something else, but that would be inhumane. I could reduce the number of seedlings of each variety of vegetable. But that would mean wasting all but two – maybe four – seeds from each seed packet.

DAY 20: The Seeds of February

So, I march outside once again for a few more inhales of icy air because obviously the first round didn't quite succeed in shaking off the delirium.

Two. I will pick two new things to try. My July-self will thank me.

Fortunately, after the catalogue over-dose, I can turn to binge-watching YouTube seed-starting videos to tide me over to the April seed-start window (for our late-May Zone 6A official start of the planting season). Of course, I can justify this obsession as (a) educational – which it is because I DO gather various tips and tricks, and (b) efficiently productive – because I listen while I do my morning kitchen cleaning/cooking routine. In the far recesses of my heart however, I know it for what it is – a crutch to get me through the next eight weeks.

Of course, my house design has no significant eastern, southern, or western exposure space that could be utilized for a seed-starting setup without blocking a sliding door or a baby grand piano. Thus, an artificial lighting system was necessary (obviously). And, I have all the parts for it. I just need to get that section of the finished basement reorganized before I set it up.

The Gardener's Spirit

But there is plenty of time for that. I know, it didn't happen last year because I got busy. But this year it will happen. Heck, it's only February.

Work. A weekend get-away. A birthday. Business income taxes. Community fund-raisers to organize, others to attend. Personal income taxes. The grandkids during school break. Easter.

Easter?! Nothing is set up. I think the seed potatoes are still in their shipping box. Where did I put last year's cucumber and zinnia seeds that I harvested? Did I really leave myself with no watermelon seeds? And the final blow, I guess I am buying herb seedlings from the nurseries this year – again.

And that is the thing about gardening – it forces me to confront the realities of time and space. Over and over again. They are inescapable.

I really do have a finite amount of time and energy and attention every day. Just because I imagine it does not mean that I have the time for it. Just because I think it would be cool does not mean that I have the space for it in my garden this year.

I get to make choices. It is a joyful limitation.

DAY 20: The Seeds of February

And this is the existential lesson of gardening – that life has limits, but I get to make choices. It is the intersection of my involvement with Nature's authority. Of my dreams, within the limits of hours of sunlight and inches of rain.

The Gardener's Spirit

Thoughts

Einstein

Look deep into nature, and then you will
understand everything better.

Cicero

If you have a garden and a library,
you have everything you need.

Thoreau

Nature will bear the closest inspection.
She invites us to lay our eye level
with her smallest leaf,
and take an insect view of its plain.

The Gardener's Spirit

DAY 21: By Hand

Kinetic. Cathartic. Energetic.

This sums up my massive weed-pulling afternoon. Massive describes both the weeds themselves and the square-footage that the weeds occupied.

Wrestling with weeds that match your height involves a lot of muscle power. Well, to be more honest in my case, I asked a lot of the little muscle that I have.

Nonetheless, after two straight hours of upside-down pulling weeds, I felt energized. My muscular engagement provided the kinetic healing balm that my sedentary body needed.

The "by hand" physical combat with pervasive roots and stubborn stems supplied the catharsis of the week's tangled emotions.

I was left renewed, restored, and centered. And grateful.

For weeds.

The Gardener's Spirit

They really do deserve more credit.

They provide us with opportunities for struggle. And, as anyone who has lived more than three decades can attest, it is an often-frustrating reality that growth and peace often come through struggle.

Pulling weeds is also, well, repetitive. Yank, toss. Yank, toss. Yank, toss, look up momentarily to note the progress. Yank, toss.

Women have long known the therapeutic nature of creative repetition – enter handcrafts such as knitting, crocheting and quilting. Men have similar activities (though less sedentary) – such as mowing the lawn and shooting hoops.

But clearing a huge patch of tall weeds takes therapeutic repetition to another level.

First, it is outside. Fresh air. Full body. Breathing deeply. And sweating.

Second, it is solitary – and private. Me against the weeds. The battle can take on any level of epic proportions that is appropriate for my emotions of the day, week, or year.

Third, it is in service to the mission of making a nurturing space for new life.

And here we have stumbled upon the heart of the matter. Why are organizing and decluttering strategies perennial favorites in the homemaking world? Because we are continually faced with the challenge of purging things in order to create nurturing spaces that support life rather than hinder it.

Human nature is hardwired to deal with the eternal conflict between chaos and order. Reference, for example, the Taoist symbol Yin-Yang, or the second theory of thermodynamics (in any system, the disorder will only increase), depending on one's proclivities.

And what better place to encounter this existential battle than the garden?

(In fact, it is almost as if a garden was the perfect place to start a story of the existential struggle of humanity in the natural world. But I digress.)

Thus, pulling weeds by hand gives me the very personal experience of bodily grappling with the nature of reality itself.

The Gardener's Spirit

And at the end of the afternoon, when I stand up and survey the land, I do not only "feel" accomplished but am accomplished. I see evidence of the successful struggle. I have space for new, nourishing life. I have a canvas to create beauty.

In restoring the garden's balance between chaos and order, I have healed my own emotional, physical, and spiritual chaos/order balance.

DAY 21: By Hand

Thoughts

The Gardener's Spirit

DAY 22: New Friends

Scientists attribute our near-universal fear of snakes to the amygdala – that small part of our brain that triggers the "fight or flight" response. Clearly, a few of us are comfortable around snakes, but I am not one of them – usually. In fact, I have mastered the art of nonchalantly bypassing the "Amphibian and Reptile House" at the zoo without the children noticing.

But this year, snakes became my friends – or, more specifically, the snakes IN MY GARDEN, became my friends.

Why? How can they be, at minimum, cringe-worthy, and at most, frightening repulsive, when behind glass at the zoo, and at the same time, in my garden be a friendly resident that elicits an "Oh, hello there" Christopher Robin-type response from me?

It started a couple of years ago when I had decided to layer my garden paths with newspapers topped with contractor-sized black garbage bags to suppress weeds and provide a semblance of order (in the absence of a mountainous supply of mulch). And then in July, as I was walking along gently tapping the Cherokee Purple tomatoes to encourage self-pollination, the black plastic moved. Quickly. In a squiggle. Traveling about two feet. Like a tremor. And then peace returned. And so did my heartbeat.

I still shake my head remembering my surprise that "they" were in "My Garden." If you are looking for true evidence of my lack of humility, then look no further than my presumption that my Earthly garden would not include snakes, when the Master of the Universe's Garden did. (I know, I know. My arrogance embarrasses me too.)

To clarify, the snakes in my neck of the US Northeast Zone 6A are of the mostly friendly variety. In fact, you would be hard-pressed to encounter one of my state's two poisonous snakes (Eastern Copperhead and Timber Rattler) as they rarely make their appearance, and their venom is seldom deadly.

No, my squiggly garden residents were the "average" Eastern Garter snake. Note that confusion still abounds about the snake's name – we continually ask our friends, "Is it called a garden snake or a garter snake, or are those two different things?" Of course, did I ask a friend? Nope, not me. Instead, I immediately searched online for that answer, because (as previously discussed) "phoning a friend" would

DAY 22: New Friends

have required a level of humility that I have not yet attained (sometimes I feel like I am perpetually enrolled in the "Remedial Humility 050" course). Upon reflection, I realized that the black plastic provided them with shade (and warmth) as well as with moisture (and respite from it).

A few weeks later, I found a snakeskin. So, I knew that they were residing comfortably enough in my garden habitat to stay a while.

Then, a while later, I moved a pile of newspapers (that I had left to decompose in place), and one looked up at me with annoyance. I had disrupted his quiet dark room with light and noise during an otherwise tranquil afternoon siesta. I apologized for my intrusion, replaced the newspapers, and realized that I needed to start being not just aware, but also considerate of, my fellow residents.

From then on, I was no longer surprised when the black plastic moved, or the leafy mulch swished, or a something streaked stage left when I approached a flower (or weed) bed. In fact, I welcomed the encounters.

I appreciate them – and like to believe that they appreciate me too (*see* the above-noted Christopher Robin approach to communication and anthropomorphizing). I provide them with shelter and food (in the form of the other garden creatures), and they provided me, well, with a full-circle form of community by balancing my slug and frog population. I hear that they could also be fond of worms, but I choose to ignore that rumor.

And now, I happily welcome my new friends' fleeting presence, and the discovery of their eggs and discarded skins. They are part of the garden family. And, not a disliked, exiled member of the family either. More like the family introvert who does not necessarily attend the family gatherings with the birds and the bees and the flowers and the trees, but one who nonetheless appears now and then with a treasured book or a classic vinyl album.

They complete the garden habitat.

In so doing, they keep me grounded in the truth of life on Earth: I cannot manipulate the fabric of reality into being composed of only the happy flowers, butterflies and praying mantis. The slugs – and the snakes – offer their weft to the warp. Without both, the fabric cannot exist.

DAY 22: New Friends

Thoughts

The Gardener's Spirit

DAY 23: Chaos and Order

Despite less than thorough research, I present here my shocking conclusion about rocks:

No two rocks are alike.

Of course, this opinion evolves only from sparce anecdotal evidence, because contrary to my feelings, my multiple bent spades and my broken garden fork, I have not yet encountered every rock in my garden, never mind the world.

However, despite my albeit limited evidence, I believe my conclusion to be nonetheless accurate.

Not only are they each uniquely shaped, but they are also chaotically arranged. Do I ever find them in an orderly line? No, not at all. I find them vertical and horizontal, above, and below, here and there – with the emphasis on HERE, where I want to plant THIS seedling.

Given all these qualities, I would be inclined to conclude that rocks clearly fall in the Chaos Camp.

But then, I know that to be untrue.

Rocks reveal patterns – and structure.

Do I spy, with my little eye, the root of a weed? And a worm? Then guaranteed there is a rock waiting below.

Are there healthy plants in a bed that contained big rocks at the start of the season? If so, then the soil will have soft rich soil and small rocks by season's end.

Let us not forget the rock walls (made from the unearthed monsters) that protect the tender sprouts from the four-footed visitors (or at least some of them), provide a shady space for our snake friends, and furnish a favorite party place for our underground earthworm friends.

So, should I therefore relocate rocks into the Order Camp?

And it was at this point that it hit me – Every aspect of Nature masterfully blends Chaos and Order.

Rocks do not have a monopoly on this Chaos/Order duality. Flowers, birds, and the rain similarly impose their duality on my garden constantly.

DAY 23: Chaos and Order

If Nature exhibited too much Order, I would not struggle to have it bring forth the veggies and herbs that I desire. I could apply a linear formula, and a consistent, dependable result would follow.

If Nature produced too much Chaos, the continual failure and destruction would prevent me from having the will even to attempt the task.

So, if gardening forces me to wrestle with this ever-present duality of Chaos and Order, then is the Divine trying to teach me something about it?

If so, what am I supposed to learn from this duality?

Perhaps the lesson is that I am in fact tasked with keeping the opposing forces in balance.

Of course, I favor this lesson – as it puts me in control. However, several decades of life lessons make me suspect that me being in control is probably the opposite of a Divine path to wisdom. (But one can dream.)

Perhaps the lesson is that I am merely asked to embrace this duality, addressing it as it presents itself.

Once again, I suspect this might be the correct answer on the Cosmic multiple-choice quiz. And once again, my humanity resists filling in that oval with every fiber of my being because living with paradox is unsettling.

Perhaps the answer is "All of the above." The garden provides a perfect opportunity to wrestle with one of the most glorious as well as the most painful realities of life – that we mortals have some influence at some times, in some places, and have absolutely no influence at other times and places.

In my garden, I can choose to cultivate a bed of colorful cosmos that will offer a plethora of nectar and pollen for the honeybees. But I may not be able to prevent the deer from eating the tender buds before they bloom, or the endless rains from spreading a lethal mildew that wipes them out.

I can observe the patterns of the rocks' interaction with weed roots and worms, and I can build rock walls. But I may not be able to dictate the rate at which the soil's biology turns those rocks into minerals that will feed my tomato plant.

And this, in and of itself, must be the reason why I relax when I am working in my garden. I am suspended in a type of meditation that welcomes the routine of activity, enjoys the suspense of the discoveries that await me, and thrives (admittedly

DAY 23: Chaos and Order

after the occasional grumbling) on the challenges that Nature's Chaos and Order present.

And when I leave the garden, I am centered. And grateful. Oh, that is the lesson.

The path to Divine centeredness and gratitude lies in the intentional engagement with Nature's Dance of Order and Chaos.

(Turns out, it was not a multiple-choice question after all.)

Thoughts

DAY 24: Crickets

My relationship with crickets differs significantly from that with grasshoppers.

Despite my childhood affection for them thanks to their summer night serenades and Pinocchio's Jiminy Cricket, their hostile takeover of my garden this year has resulted in my renewed appreciation of the popular axiom, "The enemy of my enemy is my friend."

Truth be told, it is I, not the crickets, who is the source of my current garden problem. I am after all, the one who allowed the weeds to take over sizable portions of my garden.

And not just ordinary tame weeds like dandelions or chickweed. No. I allowed four-foot square blocks of mugwort to grow chest-high. I further deluded myself into believing that a perimeter of thick mugwort made a brilliant "deer fence."

While the mugwort did create a deterrent for the deer, it also furnished the crickets with a moist, sheltered haven, shaded from the heat of the summer sun. Little did I know that crickets could consume an entire bed of newly planted SEEDS as soon as I turned my back.

I had been wrongly accusing the usual suspects – those adventurous chickens and peacocks who regularly hopped their fence for an evening stroll through the garden. Alternatively, thinking the seeds may have had a zero percent germination rate, I replanted.

As our summer days continued for weeks at the 90-degree mark into August (much longer than usual in my Zone 6a), I began to witness the presence of crickets during the cooler hours. Then the sound of their abundant chirping. Then their increased proliferation. Everywhere.

The connection between the crickets and the disappearing seeds did make itself immediately known. Rather, their presence in every patch of the garden prompted me to research – of course. (Research is my go-to salve for all things gardening. Who are we kidding? Research is my default response to everything. It is part of my continuing delusion that arming myself with enough facts will solve all my problems.)

And, lo and behold, a cricket's favorite food group is – SEEDS.

DAY 24: Crickets

Now, one would think that the consequences of these crickets' dietary preferences would not be that great given that it was now late August/early September and nearing the end of the season. But that would be an incorrect conclusion because I had, in fact, made an aggressive move into sowing winter cover crops much earlier (September) and more abundantly than I had the prior year (which had been my winter cover crop inaugural year).

We are talking whole twelve-foot by twelve-foot patches of a winter rye, tillage radish, hairy vetch, and Austrian pea mix. The stalwarts of the winter cover crop world. They were going to ensure that my spring beds were rich, loamy, earthworm-filled welcoming committees for next year's seeds and seedlings.

Having patted myself on the back for improving upon my prior year's experiences and thus advancing my gardening skills, I was now confronted with Nature's humbling lessons – again.

And so it was that three weeks after the second sowing of the cover crop mix, only a few sprouts made their appearance. And now armed with my research, I turned and shot an indisputably withering glare at the plump crickets lounging among the mugwort.

The Gardener's Spirit

And they, in reply, smirked, glanced at the mugwort, and summarily directed me to my mirror. (And after a brief moment in said reflection, I began negotiations with the frogs and the birds, the enemies of my enemy.)

DAY 24: Crickets

Thoughts

The Gardener's Spirit

DAY 25: Bees and Lavender

I have always enjoyed watching bees busily move among flowers, regardless of whether they are my cosmos or my cucumber flowers.

But then I planted lavender. And the bees arrived the following year.

None of my previous bee-watching in the garden adequately prepared me for the experience. If you have not yet encountered bees on lavender, invite yourself to a friend's lavender patch in July.

First, let us just note for a moment the intoxication that is a lavender patch. One lavender plant is nice. As a perennial, it takes at least a year to get settled into its new home and grow into its strong yet delicate fullness. But as a patch, lavender is a presence more than it is a plant.

Your eye is immediately drawn to the undulating shades of purple, which you then notice, are perfectly accented by an essence of green vibrations. The visual and emotional effects are similar to those captured by Monet in his Water Lilies W.1661 painting.

And then, the fragrance enchants you. And like a benevolent aromatic version of Odysseus' sirens, it calls you to linger. Just a little longer. As if insisting that you could merge with it and become part of its presence.

But, when I encountered the lavender patch laden with bees, well, it mesmerized me in a profound way. Before me swayed an entire palette of purple with its heady aroma, emanating a full spectrum of humming created by the maze of bees within it.

Sight, scent, sound all combined to complete the suspension of time and space.

In fact, only after its enchantment had lifted, did I realize that I could barely see the individual bees, so enmeshed were they within the multitude of tiny flowers.

And I found myself jealous. Jealous of bees at one with lavender.

They had merged with the lavender's intoxicating presence. They could not only linger but interact with it. But still, it was more than that. The bees' engagement had elevated the lavender's entire presence. It was no longer just a plant or even a patch.

DAY 25: Bees and Lavender

It had transformed into a new entity – one that opened a door to the profound.

Much like Olympic athletes do in the moment of victory. They have the same human elements as the rest of us. But they have developed all the human pieces into a being that can create a transcendent experience. And when we witness it, we can feel the sparks of the earthly realm touching the Divine.

And so, when I came upon the bees engaged with the lavender patch, the sight, the scent and the sound all combined to open the doorway to the Divine, if only just a crack, for only just a moment.

Neither the lavender nor the bees created the transcendent quality, but rather it was the intertwining of their aligned unique strengths that transformed them into a new entity. Fortunately for us, unlike the Olympics, the bees and the lavender are allowed to meet more than once every four years. In fact, arranging the time and place for the meetings is well within our gardeners' abilities.

All that is left for me to do is to remember to pause and give witness to the transformation. And that brings me to my constant reminder that gardening's value for me lies not just in the "doing" (and the tomato sandwiches). It also (and more importantly)

The Gardener's Spirit

gives me the chance to experience the Divine door opening a little, and to be transformed by it.

DAY 25: Bees and Lavender

Thoughts

The Gardener's Spirit

DAY 26: A little every day

I have many talents. Pacing myself is not one of them. When it comes to a project that combines curiosity and creativity, I am a jump-into-the-deep-end-of-the-pool-with-both-feet sort of person.

So, of course, in my mind I imagined planting all 2,000 square feet of my new garden in one big effort in one day. Maybe one weekend.

I thoroughly enjoyed the work, the digging, the planting. And then, eight hours later, I looked up and four feet of one row were planted.

In truth, the in-ground (not raised) beds did not yet exist. I was creating them three inches at a time with each spade of compacted dirt and rocks – not soil – that I dug out and filled with a young seedling. I emptied ten-foot squares of weeds and rocks to create the future perfect pumpkin, butternut squash and watermelon patches.

Weeds arrived seemingly overnight – and in abundance. May turned into June, the days became warmer, and my "to do list" grew longer. My vision of a long walk down beautiful and bounteous garden paths resigned to the reality of the energy and hours needed to transform 2,000 square feet of dirt, rocks and weeds into a vibrant garden thriving in healthy soil.

And so it was that when I would start preparing to go to the garden, a 20-minute drive from my house, I found myself tempted not to go.

I had plenty of "good" reasons not to go –
- I wouldn't have enough time to get all the things done that I wanted to do. So, I'll go when I have more time.
- I wouldn't have enough energy to get all the things done that I wanted to do. So, I'll go when I have more energy.
- I don't have all the supplies gathered for all the things that I wanted to do. So, I'll spend my time gathering the supplies, and then I'll go when I am more prepared.

It is amazing how our emotions and brain can team up to turn against us and rob us of our greatest joy. What is that called? Oh yeah, self-sabotage, the spirit of self-destruction. Sometimes referred to as The Enemy who comes to steal, kill and destroy. The Enemy is my destructive inner whisperings that

DAY 26: A little every day

prompt my worst self to lie to my best self – and steal my best future.

In a fortunate moment of recognizing this, I forced myself to go to the garden despite not having "enough" time, "enough" energy, or "enough" preparation. And the strangest thing happened. Despite my imperfect appearance in the garden, it renewed me.

Just showing up, imperfectly, doing a little piece, transformed me from a stressed, tired, grumpy task-driven maniac into a happy, content, grounded human being. Clearly, we are in miracle territory, far beyond my understanding. But perhaps we can pull back the curtain just a bit and investigate, as gardeners are expert at doing.

One thing I realized was that when I am trying to "squeeze in" a trip to the garden, I am in my To Do List mode. Everything gets weighed in terms of efficiency, priorities, time allocation, etc. So, mentally, I think I am going to the garden to "plant 10 tomatoes and 16 flowers and set up 2 cucumber trellises and spray Deer Out around the green beans and mulch the echinacea."

But in truth, when I show up imperfectly at the garden, i.e. with the time, energy and materials to do only a fraction of that To Do List, I do not put my nose to the grindstone and myopically focus on my list of chores. Instead, I make an initial walk through the garden. I say "Hi" to the cosmos and the zinnias as I reach out to gently brush them, noting that there are a few buds where there were none before. I bend down to whisper encouragement to the newly sprouted zucchini seedlings. I look up at the sky and breathe.

Then I spot the goats who are watching me, wondering when I will bring them a snack of weeds. I promise to drop some in their corral upon my departure. And then I pick up the one tomato seedling in its red plastic cup, and walk down the path to its destination, with a trowel and knee cushion in hand, humming.

It becomes an experience, not a To Do List checkmark. In fact, it's an experience during which I exhale. My husband recently made an excellent observation about my breathing. I was getting all worked up about something and he suggested we take a deep breath to calm down. So, we did. And then he said, "Exhale Tree, exhale. Exhaling is an important part of breathing."

In the garden, I don't need to remind myself to exhale. Anything that can get me not only to exhale, but to do it automatically, is a winning experience in my life.

DAY 26: A little every day

After a few "imperfect and minor accomplishments" trips to the garden, I realized that I had created a pattern of "doing a little every day." For a "jump-in-the-deep-end" person, this is a revolutionary habit. And before my eyes, the garden came to life. A little every day.

Now I understand. Now I just show up. I go to the garden with my current energy, some supplies, and an idea of a few places to start. I accept that this year's garden will flourish as much as my time, energy, and supplies allow in the face of that which is beyond my control – nature.

And I will flourish with it. I will grow transformative habits – a little every day. Including exhaling.

The Gardener's Spirit

Thoughts

DAY 27: Baked Dirt

When my gardening goals outgrew my HOA-regulated backyard, I shifted my gardening activities to raised beds in community gardens. Fortunately, in my library wanderings through the Dewey-decimal 700's, I stumbled upon the original 1981 "Bible" of raised bed gardening – Mel Bartholomew's *Square Foot Gardening* (still worth reading for its insightful commentary on the differences between farming and home-gardening, as well as for its raised bed strategies.)

And thanks to Mel, my raised bed gardens flourished. How could they not? The Square Foot Gardening ("SFG") method operated on perfect squares within perfect squares within perfect squares. It was a math nerd's dream. If you are not familiar with the now-famous SFG-method, it consists of making a grid of one-foot squares in your raised bed and then dividing each square into 2, 4, 6, 8 or 9 smaller squares (depending on the vegetable being grown) and planting a seed in each.

Actually, two seeds in each – in case one doesn't sprout.

Beyond the unique grid layout, Mel had also developed a specialized method of planting the seeds. Instead of inserting seeds into bare soil (or per the SFG book, into the "Mel's Mix" that filled the raised bed), Mel's secret was to plant the two seeds into a small hole filled with vermiculite (a natural substance that retains moisture extremely well, without getting soggy). And Mel's secret delivered amazing germination rates in my raised bed gardens.

Fast forward several years and I found myself in the third year of gardening on the farmland with four things happening simultaneously:
- I couldn't find vermiculite in my local stores and thus (wrongly) assumed that its production had been stopped.
- I didn't want to use raised beds because my true goal was to grow awesome soil (with my baseline soil being very compacted).
- I thought (again wrongly) that if farmers could make things grow by "tossing seeds" into a furrow from the back of a tractor, then I should be able to do the same without "cheating" with vermiculite.

DAY 27: Baked Dirt

- I decided to plant the entire 2,000-square-foot lot instead of just the small section I had been planting.

It was a formula for disaster.

I started with a tilled field (previously covered with weeds). But, because I had left it unattended for a while in the spring, it became brittle and covered with rocks. It took a few weeks, but I eventually was able to wrestle the rocks into a pile, dug the eight-inch-wide holes, tossed in some compost, and planted my tomatoes and peppers.

That strategy worked fine for the transplants. But my seeds were a different matter.

When I had planted only a corner of the plot in prior years, I had used Mel's vermiculite-filled-holes for planting the cucumber and bush bean seeds.

But now, being in my third year at the in-ground garden, I had mistakenly believed that the soil would have improved to the soft lush loam of a newly filled raised bed. And so, I turned my back on Mel's vermiculite approach to planting the seeds. After all, wasn't I "babying" the seeds? If acres of farmers' corn

The Gardener's Spirit

seeds can handle the rugged furrows, surely my few beans, cukes and lettuce seeds could handle being hand-sprinkled directly into a little indent in the ground. Oh, the delusions of a perfectionist gardener.

I prepared the bed – removing the early spring weeds, adding some form of compost, and creating a nicely moist surface that awaited the flat white oval seeds of future cucumbers, dark round seeds of future string beans and specks of dust – a.k.a. lettuce seeds.

My fingers rippled through the deceptively cooperative soil before placing, dropping and sprinkling the seeds at their required depths. I patted the soil, fortified it with a liberal swig of water, and whispered a plea and a wish.

With the seeds nestled into their summer homes, I considered how best to keep the soil moist during that ever sensitive 7-to-14-day germination period.

In a raised bed, the soil is softer, less rocky, and less exposed. It is also easier to water and keep moist – spray the hose a few feet here and a few feet there, and we're done. Plus, rarely is an entire raised bed's surface at the mercy of the sun. Usually, we have some transplants in the raised beds which keep the soil

DAY 27: Baked Dirt

cooler and moister, thus assisting the germinating seeds.

But with bare ground, in a large space, operating mostly in beds that may be slightly mounded, but not raised, transplants are rarely interplanted among a seeded row.

And using traditional mulch to retain moisture isn't a viable solution as it often gets blown or washed onto the new sprout at precisely the wrong moment, thus destroying it. I would use straw for mulch because it really does have the perfect structure and texture for seed sprouting. But since I continue to hear horror stories of entire gardens devastated by persistent herbicide-contaminated straw, I rejected that option.

I could water every day (a somewhat unrealistic plan given that it's a one-hour job on a 2,000-square-foot garden that's almost a half hour away). Or it could rain. Or, we could have a hot, dry May – in fact, a six-week drought – that baked the soil every day by noon (which of course is exactly what happened). By the end of June, the soil had reverted to dirt. And not just dirt but baked dirt.

The seeds that didn't get fried got eaten by birds.

The Gardener's Spirit

And so it was, in that third year, that gardening taught me:

- In-ground garden beds really do need much more preparation and attention than raised beds. They need a fall prep (not just spring plowing) that involves compost and cover crops and/or heavy-carbon-based mulch. They need EARLY spring prep that involves weed-pulling and more compost and mulch – and even perhaps an early spring cover crop and/or veggie crop.
- If the seeds get planted too late in spring, then they need to be watered daily, or planted near shade/moisture-companion plants, or even possibly, replaced with transplants.
- Baked dirt is the nemesis of every gardener – and farmer. If farmers don't irrigate during a six-week drought, then they have the same baked dirt issue that I had – unless they've been building their soil as expertly as Gabe Brown has in his regenerative ag approach. But I don't have cows, and I'm not as expert as he is. (Nonetheless, my heart's desire is to deeply improve this plot's soil using a no-till (since year 3) and chemical/pesticide-free approach to soil-building).

DAY 27: Baked Dirt

- Vermiculite is not "babying" the seeds or cheating. There is no cheating in gardening. Cheating is for tests. Gardens are for fun, beauty, and experimenting. (Obviously, this is news to me; I thought everything was a test.)
- Gardening a diverse combination of vegetables, annual/perennial flowers, and cover crops across 2,000 square feet is an entirely different challenge than planting and maintaining 400 square feet of some tomatoes and cucumbers.
- Farmers have different strategies that don't work for me – and vice versa. For example, I have deer and groundhogs that could easily wipe out my entire garden crop (and thus require making adjustments that farmers could not and do not consider). Farmers have those pests too (and more), but those four-legged pests don't usually eat the whole ten acres. So, I am not limited in how I approach my soil-building and gardening goals. I am free to experiment in any way that I think will work for my goals.
- My gardening goals change from year to year – as do my life goals, my schedule, and my priorities. As does the weather. Given all that change, my gardening "progress" will be serpentine, not linear.

The Gardener's Spirit

That year, now affectionately known as the "Baked Dirt Season," opened my eyes to a lot of realities that I would not have otherwise considered. If I were to sum them up, it would be this:

1. Life doesn't go as planned.

2. Adjusting the plan early and often yields better results.

3. Keep the true goal in mind.

As to that last part, of course I love the perfectly ripened Cherokee Purple tomatoes from my garden. But my true gardening goals? Happiness, enjoyment, centeredness, balance, fun, joy – oh, and happy earthworms and deep, rich soil.

DAY 27: Baked Dirt

Thoughts

The Gardener's Spirit

DAY 28: Experiments

I like growing vegetables and flowers. I do. But I like growing soil more. I don't know why. But having my hands in the dirt always made me happy.

So, it's no surprise that in my endless research on how to avoid cucumber viruses and combat squash bugs, I stumbled upon scientists talking about soil. They were speaking straight to my heart.

Then I found *farmers* talking about soil. And talking about it in a different way than I ever had heard before.

Farmers have different challenges than gardeners. As gardeners, we mulch and add compost. We plant the seeds gently into the soil, or vermiculite-filled holes, and cover them lovingly. We trowel out a 6-inch hole, add some perlite or peat moss or our favorite amendment like Epsom salts or calcium tablets. We gently release the seedling from its original seeding tray or its up-potted 4-inch pot, and place it in the well-prepared hole, then backfill and water it.

Not farmers. Sure, they till. They spray manure. They add NPK. But nothing close to the detailed, by-hand preparation that gardeners do.

So, here I am struggling on 2,000 square feet of garden, straight into the rock-filled ground, not wanting raised beds because I want to "grow soil," and also confused as to why farmers can have a machine make a trench, drop a seed, and corn grows, while I'm here on my hands and knees begging my carrots not to dry out while they think about sprouting.

And then I found the soil scientists who transformed the way that I looked at plants' interaction with soil. It confirmed and yet also changed some things that I had learned from SFG.

I knew the basics – earthworms, photosynthesis via the leaves, essential phosphorous and potassium and other minerals via the roots, and various nutrients released by microorganisms consuming each other.

And then I saw Dr. James White (of Rutgers University (NJ)) and Dr. Christine Jones (of Australia) on YouTube talking about root exudates

DAY 28: Experiments

and the rhizophagy cycle. And it changed my gardener's soul.

It also opened a door to an entire world of exploration about growing soil – and a new rabbit hole of research. New terms to learn. New science experiments to review. New questions to ask. New experiments to do in my own garden.

And so now, I am way past the cotton underwear disintegration soil-test experiment (although I still want to do that next year). I have already seen a huge range in my soil activity – from cardboard that lasts forever, to cardboard that disappears so completely that you only find a mysterious clue of its existence while digging a hole for a seedling, which turns out to be a remnant of the original box's packing tape.

Essentially, the scientific discovery that happened in the Ivory Tower research science world in about 2010 (that of course no one bothered to tell us mere gardeners), published by Australian researchers, while simultaneously being pursued by Dr. White, was that roots exude stuff that attracts microbes that the roots then uptake, transform and shoot out from its roots again (a.k.a. "the rhizophagy cycle").

So, the roots are not just passive recipients of the nutrients left behind by the microbes. Rather, the roots are in fact active participants in soil transformation and are responsible for orchestrating a large part of the microbial activity of the soil.

Also involved (and my research hasn't gotten this detailed yet, which is probably good because I don't think my husband could take another 2 hour one-sided "discussion" of all the cool stuff I found) is that, contrary to traditional belief, plants planted close to each other can actually manage the moisture, nutrients, and structure of the soil in a way that results in the improved growth of all the plants.

A big BUT here is that the plants must be diverse. Plant a bunch of tomato plants too close to each other and you have problems. Plant a tomato next to herbs and flowers and other veggies, and you have a symmetry going on in your soil of which I think our soil science world has just barely scratched "the surface."

So, scientific experiments, anecdotal experiences and informal farm-based experiments now abound on your favorite social media source for your viewing. Watch how farmers experimented with interplanting

DAY 28: Experiments

their winter rye with 3 other plants and found increased drought tolerance and record-breaking harvests.

My haphazard experiences with this show similar results. Last year I planted rosemary, thyme and two different flowers in a ten-inch pot. I barely watered it. It thrived. Each individual plant grew larger and more prolific than the single-species pots in the same space with the same sun and water.

When I looked closely, I realized that, if nothing else, the shade provided by the multitude of leaves kept the soil moist. Also, the roots grew through the drainage holes and into the ground.

This year's garden focused on similar interplanting (now popularly known as "companion planting"). The dill planted near the cucumbers and zucchini grew massive. The borage (and new plant for me, and a gorgeous one) and rosemary planted near the tomatoes absolutely thrived more than the ones planted solo with a twelve-inch perimeter around it.

Of course, the trade-off with this approach to gardening – that is, endless experiments – is that it takes more planning, and more researching. It

The Gardener's Spirit

borders on the complexity of creating the seating chart at a wedding. Who can't sit next to whom because they attract the same pests – or have different water needs. My rhubarb patch would have been the perfect place for my new lavender this year – except for the fact that lavender hate wet feet, while my rhubarb would prefer to live in a near-swamp.

But who are we kidding? This is exactly the type of logic problem that I live for. I just need to learn how to balance my seed-starting with my companion-planting charts and my spring bed-prep, and then maybe the garden will be planted before Independence Day.

DAY 28: Experiments

Thoughts

The Gardener's Spirit

DAY 29: Currents

When I attempt to convey to friends the common thread of my life changes over the last few years, I find that an altered title of Norman Maclean's classic book would say it perfectly - "A Garden Runs through It."

But, when it comes to the garden's life, I think Maclean's actual title, "A River Runs through It," describes the truth of the matter. Obviously, nothing grows in the garden without water, but that simple statement does not convey the scope of the matter.

Water connects every plant leaf, root, microbe and arthropod to each other. It brings life. When partnered with a plant, it transforms dirt into soil – much as the garden transforms me from a ball of tangled emotions into a centered, unified being.

Water is necessary for (a) communication between, and (b) the functioning of, everything below the soil surface. Traditionally we know that water feeds the roots. But we now also know that water is a conduit for messages between plants and soil organisms –

from root exudates to microbial activity to mycorrhizal fungi.

When I place my naked foot upon the soil, the deep, "grounded," restoration of calm can only happen with water. Dry sand or dry clay will not conduct the energy from the earth to me, nor will it take my stress and send it deep into the earth.

We are like the soil – we cannot operate without water. Scientists estimate that we are over 60% water.

But what of our bodies' electrical circuits? While we consist of water, our body also functions on electrical currents that run through our systems. And the same is true for the garden's soil. Electrical conductivity of soil is well known, regardless of the wide range of results from anecdotal experiments of encouraging additional electrical currents via copper wires, etc.

And that brings us to the eternal paradox of existence itself – or at least, another one. We must have both water and electricity to exist. So must the garden.

When we physically connect with the garden it "recharges our batteries." When we "plant" our feet in the soil, we breathe better, deeper; we calm down.

DAY 29: Currents

And our own garden is the ideal place for this – as opposed say to a forest, which is too big, too scary, too unknown. It is our own garden in which we have worked, strained, planted, and sweated, that we can become the most grounded. So, the delicate balance of water and electricity, work and rest, chaos and peace are at the core of it all.

The electricity cannot operate without the water, and yet a slight imbalance of that combination makes it ineffective at least, and deadly at most. Our lives abound with these co-existing opposites - light and dark, day and night, good and evil, turmoil and peace. In the beginning, God separated the light from the dark, the water from the land. And here we are, all these years later, our very existence still wrestling with those same essential divisions.

And so, we are left with the paradox that is at the core of human existence: navigating the delicate balance of these eternal competing forces.

Regardless of whether the garden plants are a microcosm of my physical water and electrical currents, or whether I am a microcosm of the plant world, we are connected. We have similar currents.

The Gardener's Spirit

Thus, it is no surprise that we gardeners connect with our gardens in a very fundamental way. And, as a result, our garden transforms us – not only physically but emotionally. For me, that transformation means that my essential human dualities get into balance – a rare event. That balance? That's my garden connecting me to the Divine.

DAY 29: Currents

Thoughts

The Gardener's Spirit

DAY 30: Seed Saving

As the gardening season nears its end in October, I slide into the bitter-sweet transition of letting go of all the should've, could've, would'ves – and simultaneously welcoming the cooler weather and the winter snow that it promises.

Often the work of the season and its harvest (and in some years, the work of canning and preserving the harvest) – or of the struggle with the elements that caused a lackluster harvest, leaves me exhausted and relieved that the "only" tasks remaining are pulling the plants and laying the compost and mulches.

And yet, I am uncomfortable and untethered. I will need to wait for months before I can re-connect with my soil, flowers, and burgeoning veggies. I must sit with the knowledge of this season's "losses," mulling over solution options, waiting impatiently for the opportunity to apply the curative strategies next season.

The Gardener's Spirit

But the garden gives us one lifeline that erases the sense of loss and carries us through the dark months – the seeds.

Did this year's zucchini get overgrown and ignored while you were on vacation? Fear not, take that two-foot squash and save those seeds!

Magically, what was a loss now gets moved to the win column.

Did the chipmunks eat all the fall lettuce? Let it go to seed!

Seed saving is joy and hope and restoration all in one. It is the balm that soothes all the wounds from this season in a way that our loving family cannot. They mean well. They attempt to placate us with, "There's always next year," but it barely helps.

In some magical way that I still don't fully understand, seed saving heals our wounded hearts from the season's disappointments – the promising heirloom tomatoes that got blight, the butternut squash cut down in its prime by squash vine borers, and the peas devoured by deer.

We are restored back to our original springtime optimism, despite the season's setbacks. Our eyes and heart are turned toward the future, when we will plant these little darlings in fluffy starter mix. We don't even count the number of months. Those little specks, captured in an assortment of envelopes, pill bottles and brown paper bags, blind us to yesterday's exhaustion, frustration, and impatience.

The joy of stewarding these seeds, which exist only in part from our own labors, seems to fill us with a focus and a hope that has no rival.

So, if you had a hard season, or even a good one, and you need restoration, and a dose of joy and hope, one that will buoy you through the winter months, then save some seeds – any seeds. They don't need to be your favorite tomato seeds. They don't need to be seeds from the biggest zinnias. They don't even need to be a planned event.

They can be captured when we pull the plants – grabbing them off the vine before we toss them into the compost pile. Any plants, any seeds.

We gardeners are, after all, nurturers. We love planning but embrace challenges. And our new-found seeds, especially those that come from the one remaining wilted, abandoned, pest-ravaged cucumber plant, carry us through to the spring with hope in our heart and joy in our step.

The Gardener's Spirit

Thoughts

DID YOU ENJOY THIS BOOK?

It's great to see you here! Did you enjoy this book? Did it connect with your love of gardening?

If you would be willing to help other readers and me, then I would be grateful for your review at,
Amazon https://www.amazon.com/dp/B0FSYFQDSS

and/or at Goodreads
https://www.goodreads.com/book/show/242147270.

The Gardener's Spirit

You can keep it simple and just click the stars. But, if you want to add a few words to help other readers (and me) know more about what you thought and felt, that would be wonderful!

If you would like to share your thoughts with me directly, then just email me at Theresa@TheresaMarkham.com. I appreciate your feedback because I love connecting with and encouraging gardeners through books.

GET YOUR BONUS

Get your Bonus Seed Starting Chart when you join my VIP list! https://TheresaMarkham.com/bonus-chart

The Seed Starting Chart organizes seed planting according to which seeds need:

- Light versus Dark
- Warm versus Cool temps
- Cold Stratification

When you join my VIP list, you'll receive the Seed Starting Chart – and news about upcoming books and special promotions and invitations (about once a month).

The Gardener's Spirit

BOOK & GARDENING CLUBS

Would you like to bring *The Gardener's Spirit* to your Book Club or Gardening Club?

You can get your complimentary *The Gardener's Spirit* Discussion Guide for your group – along with a bulk order discount!

Just email me at Theresa@TheresaMarkham.com about your group's size and location – and we'll get you all set up.

The Gardener's Spirit

ABOUT THE AUTHOR

The short version:
Logic and Art. Eternally intertwined.

What that looks like in real life:
Theresa Markham has been reading and writing (and playing with numbers, and drawing) since first grade. While her family is originally from two little towns outside Fall River, Massachusetts, she was fortunate enough to travel around the world as a child, thanks to her parents' adventurous spirit and her dad's service in the U.S. Army.

She was the student who actually liked writing the essays on the assigned reading in English class. (Please don't hold it against her.) Even worse, she

The Gardener's Spirit

absolutely loved math. And art. And teaching. And public speaking.

That's how she ended up at Fordham Law School in Manhattan in the 1990's, where her additional passion for research took root. And after graduation, what did she do as lawyer at Morgan Stanley in Manhattan? Yep, more research and writing. And teaching her team of attorneys. And reading, quilting, volunteering, and raising a family.

After the family moved to the farmland area of New Jersey, Theresa opened her own law firm and eventually focused on divorce law. She loved guiding her clients through one of life's most difficult challenges – and it combined her love of reading, writing, researching, problem-solving, number-crunching, public speaking – and helping people.

She homeschooled her younger daughter from 3rd grade through high school graduation (culminating in an extensive college scholarship), during which time her short-term break from the law practice became a total career change to full-time homemaker/homeschooler/volunteer. During her homemaking years, she endlessly spoiled her family and pursued lots of projects and hobbies – including gardening – and continued to use her math, art, and

ABOUT THE AUTHOR

teaching skills to tutor homeschoolers and help non-profits.

After that daughter was off to college, Theresa became a financial advisor so that she could continue to help people – but in more enjoyable circumstances than divorce. It combined her love of helping people advance and grow, her addiction to numbers, and her talent for finding creative solutions. She loves being able to have real, personal relationships with her clients.

And then she picked up gardening again. But in a different way, and at a different time in her life. It was time to stop rushing, to calm the racing thoughts and the jam-packed schedule, and to let go of at least some of the stress – and enjoy a little more happiness over the simpler things, like earthworms, and bees, and butterflies.

When she's not working with clients, she can be found doing her favorite hobby – hanging out her husband Chuck (and the kids and grandkids), as well as gardening, reading, writing, crocheting, baking, volunteering, or solving logic problems.

Most importantly, she lives in Zone 6a – where the true "last frost date" is somewhere closer to May 20th than May 10th, but the toms and cukes never go in

The Gardener's Spirit

before June 1st, and the first frost date is usually October 5th.

Thanks to the lessons of the garden, she continues to grow every day.

Got questions? Contact her at:
Theresa@TheresaMarkham.com or
https://TheresaMarkham.com